Experiencing school mathematics

Experiencing school mathematics

Teaching styles, sex and setting

Jo Boaler

Open University Press
Buckingham · Philadelphia

Open University Press
Celtic Court
22 Ballmoor
Buckingham
MK18 1XW

email: enquiries@openup.co.uk
world wide web: http://www.openup.co.uk

and
325 Chestnut Street
Philadelphia, PA 19106, USA

First Published 1997
Reprinted 1999

A catalogue record of this book is available from the British Library

ISBN   0 335 19962 3 (pb)   0 335 19963 1 (hb)

A catalog record for this book is available from the Library of Congress

Library of Congress Cataloging-in-Publication Data

Boaler, Jo, 1964–
    Experiencing school mathematics : teaching styles, sex, and setting / Jo Boaler.
        p.   cm.
    Includes bibliographical references and index.
    ISBN 0-335-19963-1 (hb). — ISBN 0-335-19962-3 (pb)
    1. Mathematics—Study and teaching (Secondary)—Case studies.   I. Title
QA11.B618   1997
510'.71'2—dc21
                                                                    97-36144
                                                                        CIP

Typeset by Type Study, Scarborough
Printed in Great Britain by St Edmundsbury Press Ltd, Bury St Edmunds, Suffolk

For Anne and Ken Boaler, with love

Contents

List of figures

List of tables

Preface

Readers should note the following points to facilitate reading.

- At various points throughout the book, numerical comparisons are made between groups of students at the two schools. Chi-squared tests were used to test for significance and where I have described groups as being 'significantly' different, this refers to a significance level of at least 1 per cent.
- The students that are quoted throughout the book were all interviewed in same-sex pairs.
- All of the names in the book of students, teachers and schools are pseudonyms. In certain interviews, 'JB' refers to the author, Jo Boaler, and after interview extracts, the students' mathematics group is given. At Amber Hill the setted ability groups are given as, for example, set 1. At Phoenix Park the different mixed-ability groups are shown by the teachers' initials.

Amber Hill staff
John Patram (JP) (head teacher)
Tim Langdon (TL) (head of mathematics)
Hilary Neville (HN) (mathematics teacher)
Edward Losely (EL) (mathematics teacher)
Liesel Harris (LH) (mathematics teacher)

Phoenix Park staff
Paul Mardon (PM) (head teacher)
Martin Collins (MC) (mathematics co-ordinator)
Jim Cresswell (JC) (mathematics teacher)
Rosie Thomas (RT) (mathematics teacher)
Barbara Burghess (BB) (mathematics teacher)
Sheila Rideout (SR) (ex-mathematics co-ordinator)
Tony Garrett (TG) (student mathematics teacher)

Acknowledgements

The teachers and students at 'Amber Hill' and 'Phoenix Park' schools made this book possible. I am profoundly grateful to the teachers at both schools, for their openness, their help and their friendship, particularly 'Hilary' and 'Tim' at Amber Hill. I would also like to record my thanks to the students at both schools.

Professor Paul Black was one of two supervisors of the PhD study that this book is based upon. Paul was a great source of support and inspiration to me and I will never forget the commitment he showed to my work. I know that I was extremely fortunate to receive the benefit of his insights which moved my thinking forward a great deal. I was fortunate also to receive the help of Mike Askew as my supervisor and I am extremely grateful to Mike for the guidance he gave me and the ways in which he informed my work. During my research study I was helped by many other colleagues at King's who unselfishly gave time to offer support and guidance. Professor Stephen Ball read through various drafts of ideas and chapters and gave me encouragement and inspiration. Professor Margaret Brown gave me important help with ideas and Dr Alison Millet and Sharon Gewirtz encouraged me with their support and friendship. I would also like to say a very special thank you to Dr Dylan Wiliam who read the entire typescript in draft form and provided me with many kinds of invaluable research advice throughout my study.

I am also grateful to Professor Leone Burton for her support and friendship over many years. I would like to thank the ESRC, whose funding made the depth of this study possible, and the two examination boards, MEG and NEAB, which gave me permission to sit and read through my students' GCSE examination papers.

Thanks also to Carfax Publishing Limited for permission to reproduce extracts of the articles that appearer in *Gender and Education* (Chapter 9) and *British Educational Research Journal* (Chapter 10).

Finally I would like to thank Colin Haysman for his unwavering support and partnership and the rest of my family who continue to inspire and encourage me.

1

Mathematics in and out of school

Introduction

'Back-to basics' policies fit comfortably within mathematics classrooms. Features such as order, control, rule-following, 'transmission' teaching and ability grouping are easy to locate within a mathematical domain and are relatively commonplace. The late 1990s have witnessed a return to favour of such 'traditional' forms of schooling, matched by a political backlash against 'progressive' educational systems. Paradoxically, perhaps, accusations about the insidious influences of progressivism are most frequently levelled at mathematics classrooms, when evidence suggests that the majority of mathematics teachers have remained faithful to the 'basic' teaching approaches now yearned for by many (Ofsted 1994).

But what do we really know about the impact of traditional practices upon the development of students' understanding? Conversely, can we be sure that 'progressive' features of classrooms such as discovery-based learning, mixed-ability teaching, independence and freedom really lead to under achievement and the lowering of standards, as many claim? Despite the strength of allegiance demonstrated by advocates of 'traditional' and 'progressive' approaches, there has been very little evidence available to inform this debate. This has led to the position we now face whereby decisions about the raising of standards are based upon memories, anecdotes and political point-scoring, rather than data, evidence or research. The aim of this book is to go some way towards changing this by examining, in detail, the experiences of 300 or so students who lived through these different teaching approaches and whose reflections and achievements stand in testimony to the effectiveness of 'traditional' and 'progressive' schooling.

In the midst of opposing claims about the relative merits of alternative teaching approaches, I conducted a detailed study of two schools, which taught mathematics in completely different ways. Funding from the Economic and Social Research Council (ESRC) enabled me to follow a year group of students in each of these schools – about 300 students in all – for three years. The two schools were chosen both because their teaching methods were completely different and their student intakes were almost identical. Up until the end of Year 8, when they were about 12 years old, students at both schools had experienced the same mathematical teaching approaches. At the beginning of Year 9, everything changed. From this point, the year group of one of the schools was taught using traditional 'chalk-and-talk' methods, whilst the year group at the other school abandoned their textbooks and worked on open-ended projects for three years. These differences reflected the philosophies of the mathematics teachers at the two schools. The two groups of students had reached the same levels of mathematical attainment up until that time, but they then experienced a substantial and important divergence in their mathematical pathways. This book tells the story of what happened to the students during these three years.

Origins of the research

Within mathematics education there is an established concern that many people are unable to use the mathematics they learn at school in situations outside the classroom context. In various research projects individuals have been observed using mathematics in real-world situations such as street markets, factories and shops. In these settings, school-learned mathematical methods and procedures are rarely used (Lave *et al.* 1984; Lave 1988; Masingila 1993; Nunes *et al.* 1993). Lave (1988) has used these research findings to challenge the traditional conception of mathematics as an abstract and powerful tool that is easily transferred from one situation to another. She has criticized theories of 'learning transfer' and sought to replace these with the idea that all learning is 'situated' (Lave and Wenger 1991: 30) and inherently linked to the situation or context in which it takes place. Lave argues that students cannot make use of the mathematics they learn in school because their mathematical knowledge is tied to the classroom situation. Lave's ideas have received strong support in the fields of anthropology, psychology and education and are now pivotal to emerging theories about human cognition. Indeed, she and others in the field of 'situated cognition' (Brown *et al.* 1989; Young 1993) have been instrumental in raising awareness of the importance of the situation, the context or the 'community of practice' (Lave and Wenger 1991) in which ideas are encountered for the knowledge that learners subsequently develop. One of the aims of this research study was to explore Lave's notion of situated learning and to investigate the experiences of students when they needed to 'transfer' mathematics from one situation to another. I was interested to discover whether different teaching approaches would influence the nature of the knowledge that students developed, and the ways that students approached new situations. In order to do this, I monitored the impact of the students' contrasting mathematical environments upon the *forms* of knowledge and understanding they developed and the effectiveness of these in different situations, including the national school-leaving examination, as well as more applied and 'realistic' tasks.

In forming my research design, I was aware that a large body of research had shown the advantages of open- or activity-based approaches to mathematics teaching for students' performance on tests (Athappilly *et al.* 1983; Resnick 1990; Maher 1991; Sigurdson and Olson 1992; Keedy and Drmacich 1994).

However, there appeared to be very little research that examined the nature and form of the classroom processes that contributed towards differential achievement. My aim therefore was not only to monitor the effectiveness of two schools' approaches, but to examine the intricate and complex ways in which the different approaches influenced students. In order to achieve this I conducted in-depth, longitudinal and ethnographic studies of students working within their own school environments.

The story that will be told in this book concerns the mathematics teaching and learning in two schools. But this is not just an account of different mathematics approaches, it is also about different educational systems, popularly characterized as 'traditional' and 'progressive'; about setting and mixed-ability teaching; about gender and learning styles and about the ways that these factors play out in the day-to-day experiences of students in classrooms. The messages that emerged from the two schools were varied and, at times, unexpected. My ability to tell the story and to communicate the systematic differences between the teaching methods derives from the clear and open ways in which students reported their experience of the learning process. The students that are portrayed in this book will take the reader some way towards the worlds of school mathematics as they experienced them. The descriptions that the students provided of their learning experiences will be combined with descriptions of their actions, behaviours and understandings to give insights into the links between teaching approaches and student understanding. The fact that this research is focused upon two schools raises questions about its generalizability, but I am happy for these questions to be raised and for the answers to be sought within the pages of this book.

2

The schools, students and research methods

In the chapters that follow, the schools and the students will be described in some depth. The purpose of this chapter is to give a brief introduction to the two research settings, the students within them and the methods used to monitor and understand their experiences.

Research methods

In order to contrast two different mathematical approaches, I conducted ethnographic, three-year case studies (Eisenhart 1988) of the mathematical environments in two schools. As part of these case studies, I performed a longitudinal cohort analysis of a year group of students in each school as they moved from Year 9 (age 13) to Year 11 (age 16). I followed the same students for three years, monitoring their different learning experiences over time. The two case studies included a variety of qualitative and quantitative methods, and an overview of the research methods, used is given in the Appendix (page 8). I chose to combine these different research strategies, partly because of a belief that qualitative and quantitative techniques are not only compatible, but complementary. I also used a number of different techniques in an attempt to represent what Ball (1995: 259) has termed the 'mobile, complex, ad hoc, messy and fleeting qualities of lived experience'. Ball (1995) and Miles (1982: 126) both warn of the danger of reducing the complexity of experience and striving towards a theory that it 'all makes sense'. In analysing the practices of two schools I did not wish to provide a definitive explanation of events, but a way of thinking that raised issues and questions about various features of school life. To this end, my research design was governed by the need to view events from a number of different perspectives and to conceptualize factors such as enjoyment and understanding in different ways.

To understand the students' experiences of mathematics, I observed approximately 90 one-hour lessons in each school, usually taking the role of a 'participant observer' (Kluckhohn 1940; Eisenhart 1988). I interviewed 32 students in Year 10 and 44 students in Year 11; I analysed comments elicited from students and teachers about classroom events (Beynon 1985); I gave questionnaires to all of the students in my case study year groups each year;

I interviewed teachers at the start and end of the research and I collected an assortment of background documentation. These methods, particularly the lesson observations and student interviews, enabled me to develop an understanding of the students' experiences and to begin to view the worlds of school mathematics from the students' perspectives (Hammersley 1992). In order to locate the students' perspectives within a broad understanding of the two schools I also spent time 'hanging out' (Delamont 1984) in the staffrooms and the corridors of the schools, I socialized with staff and I tried to develop a sense of the two schools in as many ways as possible.

In addition to these methods, I gave the students various assessments during the three-year period. Most of these I designed myself but I was also given permission to visit the examination boards used by the two schools and conduct a detailed examination of the students' General Certificate of Secondary Education (GCSE) examination responses. The various assessment activities and questions I used during the three years involved individual and group work, written and practical work. All of the research methods employed within the study were used to inform each other in a continual process of interaction and re-analysis (Huberman and Crandall 1982). Observation data were collected and analysed using a grounded theory approach (Glaser and Strauss 1967) and fieldnotes and interviews were analysed through a process of open coding (Strauss and Corbin 1990).

The students involved

The overall aim of my research study was to monitor the experiences of a year group of students as they moved from Year 9 to Year 11, but constraints of time meant that some of my research methods needed to be focused upon particular groups of students within the two year groups. For example, my lesson observations, interviews and 'applied' assessments could not be conducted with all of the mathematics groups in each year because of the time required by these methods. At the more traditional school, which I have called 'Amber Hill', the year group was divided into eight 'ability' groups (sets 1–8) who were all taught mathematics at the same time. I therefore decided, at an early point in my study, to focus some of my data-collection methods upon sets 1–4. This decision was not made because I was particularly interested in 'high ability' students. The decision was made mainly because the head of mathematics was most comfortable with me visiting these groups and partly because the students in sets 1–4 demonstrated some interesting patterns of performance in the first applied assessment activity I gave them. I therefore decided that most, but not all, of my lesson observations for my case study year group, would be of sets 1–4, and only those students (who I came to know well) would take applied assessments. In my observations of other year groups at Amber Hill, I observed students in the full range of sets (1–8).

At the more 'progressive' school, which I call 'Phoenix Park', there were five mixed-ability mathematics groups who were taught mathematics at different times of the day. This meant that I could watch up to three of my case study year group lessons in one visit to Phoenix Park and I did not need to focus my methods upon particular groups. My lesson observations, interviews and assessments involved all five groups. When I was not observing lessons with my case study year group, I watched lessons in other year groups.

All other research methods, including questionnaires, short assessment questions, observations of other year groups and GCSE analyses were carried out with the full range of groups in each school.

Initial entry measures

At the beginning of my research study, when the students were just starting Year 9, I analysed the results of National Foundation for Educational Research (NFER) tests which both schools had administered to all their students at the beginning of Year 9. These were mathematics tests, focusing in particular upon numeracy. NFER provide national results for these tests, so I was able to standardize the results of both schools. The results for these tests are given in Table 2.1. The results of these tests showed that there were no significant differences between the two schools and that 75 per cent of Amber Hill students and 77 per cent of Phoenix Park students were below the national average for the test.

I also administered my own set of questions to the case study year groups at both schools. These were seven contextualized questions assessing various aspects of number work. The results for these questions are given in Tables 2.2–2.4. Grade 1 is the correct answer in each case. There were no significant differences between the two schools on any of these questions. At the beginning of Year 9, the students therefore appeared to have reached very similar levels of attainment, measured on a broad range of mathematics questions.

Note

1 Forty of the Amber Hill students did not take this test (due to student absence and general student turn-over). Of these students 17 went into sets 1–4, 23 went into sets 5–8.

Table 2.1   Standardized NFER scores (mean = 100, standard deviation = 15). For Amber Hill, n = 160; for Phoenix Park, n = 109[1]

School	73–81	82–91	92–101	102–111	112–121	122+
Amber Hill	40 (23%)	40 (25%)	40 (25%)	25 (16%)	12 (8%)	3 (2%)
Phoenix Park	18 (17%)	38 (35%)	27 (25%)	18 (17%)	6 (6%)	2 (2%)

Table 2.2   Number difference problem in two contexts (per cent)

	'Chocolate splits'		'Tug of war'	
Grade	Amber Hill	Phoenix Park	Amber Hill	Phoenix Park
1	49	41	49	43
2	53	54	44	47
3	8	5	5	1
4	1	1	3	1
n	195	110	195	110

Table 2.3   Number group problem in two contexts (per cent)

	'Cutting wood'		'Fashion workshop'	
Grade	Amber Hill	Phoenix Park	Amber Hill	Phoenix Park
1	58	55	57	60
2	19	28	23	23
3	17	13	11	12
4	6	4	9	6
n	195	110	195	110

Table 2.4   Addition of fraction problem in three contexts (per cent)

	'Penalties'		'Plants'		Abstract	
Grade	Amber Hill	Phoenix Park	Amber Hill	Phoenix Park	Amber Hill	Phoenix Park
1	3	6	2	4	1	1
2	3	1	3	2	7	7
3	93	92	94	91	81	83
4	1	1	2	4	10	9
n	195	110	195	110	195	110

Appendix Research methods used in the study

Time	Research method	Subjects involved
Year 9		
Term 1	Interviews	Four teachers from Amber Hill
		Three teachers from Phoenix Park
	Seven contextualized short assessment questions	All year group in both schools, $n = 305$
Term 2	Lesson observations One full week in each school	Approximately 25 lessons in each school
	Questionnaires (including open and closed questions)	All year group in both schools, $n = 263$
Term 3	'Applied Architectural' activity and tests	Half of four groups in each school, $n = 104$
	Lesson observations	Approximately five lessons per school
Year 10		
Term 1	Lesson observations	Approximately ten lessons per school
Term 2	Long-term learning tests	Two groups in each school, $n = 61$
	Lesson observations One full week in each school	Approximately 25 lessons per school
Term 3	Seven contextualized short assessment questions	All year group in both schools, $n = 268$
	Questionnaires (including open and closed questions)	Years 9, 10 and 11 in both schools, $n = 653$
	Interviews	16 students each from Amber Hill and Phoenix Park
	'Applied Flat Design' activity and tests	Four groups in each school, $n = 188$
	Lesson observations	Approximately ten lessons per school
Year 11		
Term 1	Lesson observations One full week in each school	Approximately 25 lessons per school
Term 2	Interviews	24 students from Amber Hill, 20 from Phoenix Park
	Questionnaires (closed responses only)	All year group in both schools, $n = 202$
	Interviews	Three teachers from each school
	Lesson observations	Approximately five lessons per school
Term 3	Analysis of GCSE answers	All GCSE entrants in each school, $n = 290$

3

An introduction to Amber Hill and Phoenix Park schools

Introduction

Both Amber Hill and Phoenix Park schools lie in the heart of mainly white, working-class communities located on the outskirts of large cities. Both schools are surrounded by council-owned houses where the majority of children live. Neither school is selective, and most parents choose the schools for their proximity to their houses. In an analysis of socio-economic status, derived from fathers' occupations, there were no significant differences between the case study year groups in the two schools. Amber Hill is a secondary school which begins with Year 7, when students are 11 years of age. There were about 200 students in the year group I followed: 47 per cent of these were girls, 20 per cent were from single-parent families, 68 per cent were classified as working class and 17 per cent were from ethnic minorities. Phoenix Park is an upper school and the students start in Year 9 when they are 13 years of age. There were approximately 110 students in the year group that I followed: 42 per cent of these were girls, 23 per cent were from single-parent families, 79 per cent were classified as working class and 11 per cent were from ethnic minorities. A comparison of the initial attainment of the students revealed that there were no significant differences between the students at the beginning of Year 9 (see Chapter 2).

Amber Hill school

Amber Hill school is a mixed, 11–18-year-olds', grant-maintained comprehensive, with approximately 1200 students on roll. It is located in the main working-class area of Fieldton, a large suburb of a major city. The majority of students who attend the school are white and working-class and the school is usually placed at or near to the bottom of the league table of secondary schools in the local education authority (LEA).

The school is located in a quiet residential road, overlooked by two high-rise blocks of flats in which many of my case study students lived. One of the first things I noticed when I began my research was the apparent 'respectability' of the school. Walking into the reception area on my arrival I was struck by the tranquility of the arena. The reception was separated from the rest of the school by a set of heavy double doors. The floors were carpeted in a sombre grey; a number of easy chairs had been placed by the secretary's window and a small tray of flowers lay above them. The walls displayed photographs from sports days and school trips, awards that students had received and Amber Hill emblems and coats of arms. Icons of traditionalism were located throughout the reception area, presenting strong messages about the way in which the school was intended to be perceived.

The head teacher of Amber Hill was a particularly important and influential figure. John Patram was the archetype of the 'authoritarian head' (Ball 1987: 109), particularly in his attitude towards opposing views which were 'avoided, disabled or simply ignored'. The mathematics teachers reported that he imposed decisions upon staff, after consultations which he ignored. John Patram had an austere appearance; he was always dressed in a dark suit and wore a solemn expression. At break times he wandered the corridors shouting at students, the staff seemed as unwilling to bump into him as the students. He rarely visited the staffroom or socialized with staff.

Partly as a result of the head teacher's influence and power, Amber Hill was unusually orderly and controlled. Students generally did as they were told, their behaviour governed by numerous enforced rules and a general school ethos which induced obedience and conformity. All students were required to wear a school uniform which the vast majority of students wore as the regulations required. The annual school report encapsulated just one aspect of Amber Hill's attempts to encourage and capture an 'expressive order' (Bernstein 1966). Two boxes at the bottom of the report required the tutors to give the students a grade on their 'co-operation' and their 'wearing of school uniform'. The head teacher clearly wanted to present the school as academic and respectable and he was successful in this aim, at least in terms of the general façade. Visitors walking around the corridors would see unusually quiet and calm classrooms, with students sitting in rows or small groups, usually watching the board. When students were unhappy in lessons, they tended towards withdrawal in preference to disruptiveness. The corridors were mainly quiet and at break times the students walked in an orderly fashion between lessons. The students' lives at Amber Hill were, in many ways, structured, disciplined and controlled.

The Amber Hill staff

There were 70 teaching staff at Amber Hill who were quite polarized in terms of age. A large number of the staff had been at the school for ten years or more whilst a similar proportion were in their twenties and had been teaching for less than three years. The staff appeared to mix well although my perspective on the staff as a whole was limited by the fact that few staff spent their non-contact time in the staff room, as I, and the mathematics department, did. The remainder chose to stay within their subject domains. This tendency is indicative of teachers who fit within Bernstein's collection code (Bernstein 1971) and who have been socialized into strong subject loyalties.

The staffroom was split into two main rooms: one for smokers, the other for non-smokers. The main core of the mathematics department always sat in the smoking section, apparently because two of them smoked. The staffroom did not seem to be a particularly social place: few teachers visited it at break times, apart from the mathematics department who taught close by. Five of the mathematics department had commandeered their 'own' comfortable chairs in which they always sat. The smoking section of the staffroom tended to be a lively arena in which complaints about various students' behaviour in mathematics lessons or reports about the amount of work a student had completed would be bandied about and discussed. The mathematics department had nine members, including one teacher who worked part-time and one who taught information technology most of the time. Seven of the department had been at the school for between eight and eighteen years, two for three to four years.

The head of department, Tim Langdon, was in his mid-thirties and had been at the school for four years at the start of my research. Tim believed in the Secondary Mathematics Project (SMP) scheme, which the school used in Years 7 to 11. He regarded this to be an innovative scheme and the new publications that SMP issued from time to time made him feel that he was keeping abreast of the latest developments in mathematics education. Tim was also vocal in his support of Attainment Target 1^1 of the National Curriculum and open-ended activities, but these played a minor and compartmentalized role in the department's scheme of work, which he had designed. Tim was always friendly and amiable. He was also extremely conscientious and hard-working and would go to any lengths to help me with my research by, for example, organizing interviews, planning which lessons I could see, and sending me information and timetables.

The other teacher who helped me a great deal was Hilary Neville. Hilary was a mathematics teacher and the head of year for my case study cohort and so had a senior position in the school. Hilary was a forceful, efficient and extremely competent woman in her forties, who was both friendly and assertive with staff and students. She was also extremely committed and hard-working and obviously cared a great deal about the students. I became friends with both Hilary and Tim during my research and maintained contacts with them after my study was completed.

Edward Losely was also an important figure in the department. At the start of my research he was a newly qualified teacher of approximately 25 years of age. He was always grinning and joking with various members of staff and he helped to organize the student football and cricket teams. Edward was quite large and athletic looking and clearly enjoyed being 'one of the lads'. This extended to his lessons when he was often joking with boys in a 'laddish' way and referred to beer, pubs, football and cricket in the examples he chose to describe mathematical situations. At break times Tim, Hilary and Edward would often sit and chat about mathematics lessons and students' behaviour.

The rest of the mathematics department were aged between 40 and 60 and shared the belief that SMP was an innovative scheme. The teachers had

concerns about individual students' mathematical knowledge and understanding but they did not reveal any reservations about the SMP scheme. All
of the teachers complained to Tim about having to do investigational work
and open-ended tasks but they did believe in the occasional use of these activities.

All the mathematics teachers, Tim included, believed that the most efficient
and effective way to teach mathematics was to impart knowledge of different
mathematical procedures, using the blackboard, and then get students to practise these procedures individually. The teachers believed that if they explained
mathematical methods clearly, the students would gain an understanding of
them. The teachers also believed that students needed to do a large number
of similar exercises, because the act of repeating a procedure they had learned
would make students remember it. The teachers' belief in this didactic model
of teaching meant that their main concern as teachers was to cover all of the
necessary mathematical content:

> We've all done maths, so they've got the biggest resource standing in front
> of the class. And it's superb being able to – you've got the National Cur-
> riculum basically and if you cover the National Curriculum you're doing
> your job.
>
> (Edward Losely)

Mathematics teaching at Amber Hill

Amber Hill used the SMP scheme throughout Years 7 to 11. Within this
scheme in Years 7 and 8, the students work through individualized SMP
11–16 booklets; in Years 9 to 11, they move on to more formal textbooks.
Students spent the first term of Year 7 in mixed-ability classes and were
grouped by ability into eight mathematics sets at Christmas. The allocation
of students to sets was based upon the results of NFER tests taken at the beginning of Year 7 and work completed in the first term of Year 7. In Years 7 and
8, students worked through the individualized booklets, at their own pace,
with little or no whole-class teaching. In Year 9 they moved to a more formal
system of textbooks and class teaching. There was no departmental policy
about the way in which classes should work in Years 9 to 11, but all the
teachers adopted the same pedagogical approach. They explained methods
from the blackboard at the front of the class for the first 15 to 20 minutes of
each lesson, they then set the students questions to work through from their
SMP textbooks. Most of the teachers questioned students whilst lecturing
from the blackboard. The students worked through textbooks in every lesson
in Years 9 to 11, apart from three weeks of Years 10 and 11 when they completed an investigation or 'open-ended task'. The distinct separation of the
process and content areas of mathematics maintained within Amber Hill's
approach is what Blum and Niss (1991: 60) refer to as the 'separation
approach', common in many schools.

Most students sat in pairs in mathematics lessons, but they would work alone, usually stopping to check with their partner that they had got the same answer at the end of each question. Teachers did not object to students talking quietly as they worked. All mathematics lessons were one hour long.

JB: What do you do in a typical maths lesson?
J: Well, sir usually goes over the work we have to do before we do it. So he'll write on the board what we have to do and explain the questions and that and the rules, the basics of what we have to do in the work and then he'll tell us to get on with it.
JB: From books?
J: Yeah, from books and if we need help he'll come along and help us.
JB: And how long does he talk from the board and how long do you work from books?
J: About half a lesson.

(John, Amber Hill, Year 10, set 1)

The students worked from textbooks in each and every lesson. When they completed a chapter, they would do the textbook 'review' which assessed the work in the chapter:

A: It's always out of textbooks, innit?
G: Yeah, we do a chapter, then we do a review and it's like that over and over again.

(Alan and Gary, Amber Hill, Year 11, set 3)

Lessons at Amber Hill were unusually ordered and controlled. Students were well behaved and it was rare to see teachers invoke any disciplinary procedures against students. When the teachers talked from the front of the room, the students would sit in silence listening to them, watching the board and writing down what they were told. Students worked quietly through their exercises and confined any misbehaviour to chatting with their partners. In lesson observations I was repeatedly impressed by the work rate of the students. In a small quantitative assessment of their 'time on task' (Peterson and Swing 1982) I recorded the number of students who were working 10 minutes into, half way through and 10 minutes before the end of each lesson. Observing ten lessons, each with approximately 30 students, 100 per cent, 99 per cent and 92 per cent of the students appeared to be working at these three respective times. The first of these figures was particularly high because at this early point in lessons, the students were always watching the teachers work through examples on the board.

The students at Amber Hill wanted to do well in mathematics and believed it to be an extremely important subject. This motivation, combined with their compliant behaviour, meant that the teachers usually had captive audiences in lessons – audiences who were willing to do whatever the teachers told them. The mathematics teachers at Amber Hill had good relationships with students. All of the teachers were friendly, rather than authoritarian, and the students reported that they found them approachable and helpful.

Phoenix Park school

Phoenix Park is a mixed 13–18-year-olds' comprehensive school, located on the edge of Avadon, a prosperous town with a large middle-class element. There were approximately 600 students on the school's roll and most of the students at the school were white and working class. The majority of students lived on one of three local housing estates, one of which was infamous for its links with 'joy riding' and drug-related crimes. The school is situated in an industrial area and a large proportion of the parents used to work in the local factories before widespread redundancies were made. The juxtaposition of this working-class school next to the affluent, middle-class city of Avadon made it somewhat distinctive in the locale. It was also distinct because of a long tradition of progressive education, placing particular emphasis upon self-reliance and independence. Most of the parents who chose to send their children to Phoenix Park did so because they lived in the immediate vicinity of the school, rather than because of school philosophy or practice. In a school survey of 50 parents conducted in 1987, 44 parents said that their children lived within a 20-minute walk of the school. A few parents chose Phoenix Park because their children had special educational needs (which were given high priority in the school) and a few chose the school because of its relaxed atmosphere. This contrasted with the more pressured and academic environments of the other schools in and around Avadon. Phoenix Park, like Amber Hill, was usually placed at or near to the bottom of its LEA league table.

Phoenix Park school had an attractive 'campus' feel. The atmosphere was unusually calm, described in a newspaper article on the school as 'peaceful'. Students walked slowly around the school and there was a noticeable absence of students running, screaming or shouting. This was not because of school rules; it seemed to be a product of the school's overall ambience. I mentioned this to one of the mathematics teachers (Rosie Thomas) one day and she agreed, saying that she didn't think she had ever heard anybody shout – staff or student. She added that this was particularly evident at break times in the hall: 'The students are all so orderly, but no-one ever tells them to be.'

Phoenix Park school maintained a number of distinctive qualities, most of which derived from its commitment to progressivism. In lessons, many of the subject departments used a project-based, problem-solving approach with little, if any, recourse to textbooks. Students were taught all subjects in mixed-ability groups. Phoenix Park students did not wear school uniform. Most students wore fashionable but inexpensive clothes such as jeans, with trainers or boots, and shirts or T-shirts worn loosely outside.

A central part of the school's approach involved the development of independence amongst students. The students were encouraged to act responsibly, not because of school rules, but because they could see a reason to act in this way. In mathematics lessons, the teachers allowed the students to work on their own, unsupervised in separate rooms, as the students were expected to be responsible for their own learning. As one Year 11 student, quoted in a school publication, noted: 'You've got a lot of freedom – it's not really like a school. The teachers don't treat you like kids.'

The school had a thriving special educational needs department which it maintained throughout the late 1980s and early 1990s when many schools drastically reduced the number of teachers working within special educational needs. The school also had a commitment to equality of opportunity which extended well beyond written policy documents.

Fletcher *et al.* (1985) describe the trouble experienced by schools that attempt to be progressive in their dealings with parents. Part of the freedom Phoenix Park enjoyed in this regard seemed to be due to the working-class composition of the school and the presence of parents who were less inclined to challenge the authority of teachers. In the year after my three-year research study, the school had an influx of middle-class parents who quickly put pressure upon the teachers at the school to return to more traditional methods of schooling, including ability grouping and textbook teaching.

The Phoenix Park staff

The staff at Phoenix Park were relatively young, with approximately 30 per cent of the staff in their twenties, 30 per cent in their thirties and 30 per cent in their forties. Interactions between staff were almost always casual and jovial. In my visits to the staffroom at Phoenix Park, I was always struck by its relaxed and cheerful atmosphere. Teachers did not seem to spend their break times complaining about workload, running around organizing detentions or worrying about administration. Nor did they sit in separate subject departments talking about students who were working or not working. Instead, break and lunch times seemed to be social occasions in which staff from different departments interacted and joked with each other.

The teachers at Phoenix Park were casually dressed. One day, one of the more senior members of staff was wearing a T-shirt with the name of a rock band on it, which prompted one of the other teachers to say: 'One of the very nice things about this school is you can express yourself through your clothing!' The head teacher at Phoenix Park, Paul Mardon, did not seem distinct from other members of staff, apart from the fact that he always wore a tie. He spent his lunchtimes wandering around the school grounds chatting to students; he knew all of the students by name and they seemed comfortable in his presence.

When I began my research at Phoenix Park, the mathematics department was run by Sheila Rideout, who had a clear vision about the way mathematics should be taught. Sheila devised the mathematics approach at Phoenix Park, in conjunction with a working group of teachers adopting similar approaches in other schools. Sheila left Phoenix Park in the first year of my research and her job as mathematics co-ordinator was taken over by Martin Collins, previously her deputy. A newly qualified teacher, Rosie Thomas, was appointed to the department to restore numbers. For the rest of my research time, the department was made up of three 'and a half' mathematics teachers. Martin, Rosie and Jim Cresswell (below) all worked full-time in the mathematics department, Barbara Burghess had a part-time contract at the school.

Martin Collins, the mathematics co-ordinator, was in his mid-thirties. He had a mathematics degree and was well informed about developments in mathematics education. Martin was generally very 'laid back' about everything, including teaching mathematics and running the department. He was not an active leader and was, in many ways, the complete opposite of Sheila. He was in favour of an open approach to teaching, but he had doubts about the effectiveness of the approach they used at the school.

Jim Cresswell was unusual, particularly for a teacher of mathematics. He was in his early thirties, he had an Oxbridge degree in engineering, and he was studying Chinese at degree level in his spare time. Jim used to be a youth worker and he was a practising Quaker. He always dressed extremely casually, usually in faded jeans, a sweatshirt and in winter, a woolly hat. He had very short hair and an unshaven look. In the staffroom he was often reading books about Existentialism or Marxism. In the classroom Jim treated the students as though they were adults; he rarely ever reprimanded them and when students misbehaved he had conversations with them about the inconsiderateness of their behaviour.

Rosie Thomas was a newly qualified teacher at the start of my research. She was in her early twenties, had a mathematics degree and was enthusiastic about the school's approach and about teaching in general. She often chatted to students about mathematical and non-mathematical issues and she was generally liked by students. Rosie quickly became involved in the life of the school and she seemed to be a highly committed teacher.

Mathematics teaching at Phoenix Park

Many of the progressive principles which underscored the whole-school philosophy of Phoenix Park were represented in the mathematics approach, which made it extremely unusual. From the beginning of Year 9 to Christmas of Year 11, the students worked on open-ended projects in every lesson. During this time the students were taught in mixed-ability groups. Projects usually lasted for about three weeks. The teachers introduced students to a project or theme which the students explored, using their own ideas and mathematical knowledge. The projects were usually extremely open, amounting to little more than a challenging statement.

> The projects that we were set, we were actually given a title in the first . . . like what we had to do . . . but then after that you could decide how far you wanted to do it.
>
> (Tina, Phoenix Park, Year 11, RT)

One of the projects was called 'Volume 216'. In this project, the students were told that the volume of a shape was 216. They were then asked to go away and think about what the shape could be. Students were expected to extend their work and pursue questions and interests related to this theme. Sometimes teachers taught the students some mathematical content they thought might be needed before the start of an activity. More commonly, teachers would introduce techniques to individuals or small groups when they encountered a need for them within the particular project on which they were working.

S: We're usually set a task first and we're taught the skills needed to do the task, and then we get on with the task and we ask the teacher for help.

P: Or you're just set the task and then you go about it in . . . you explore the different things, and they help you in doing that . . . so you sort of . . . so different skills are sort of tailored to different tasks.

JB: And do you all do the same thing?

P: You're all given the same task, but how you go about it, how you do it and what level you do it at, changes, doesn't it?

(Simon and Philip, Phoenix Park, Year 11, JC)

The students were given an unusual degree of choice in mathematics lessons. When projects were introduced to them they were usually given a few ideas to choose between and when they were working on their projects they were required to decide the nature and direction of their work. Sometimes the different projects varied in difficulty and the teachers guided students towards projects that they thought were suited to their capabilities.

T: You get a choice.

JB: A choice between . . . ?

T: A couple of things, you choose what you want to do and you carry on with that and then you start another, different one.

JB: So you're not all doing the same thing at the same time?

Both: No.

JB: And can you do what you want in the activity, or is it all set out for you?

L: You can do what you want really.

T: Sometimes it's set out, but you can take it further.

(Tanya and Laura, Phoenix Park, Year 10, MC)

The pedagogy of Phoenix Park would be ideally described in Bernstein's (1975: 116) terms as 'invisible' because:

- the teachers had implicit rather than explicit control over students;
- the teachers arranged the *context* in which students explored work;
- students had wide powers over the selection and structure of their work and movements around the school;
- there was reduced emphasis upon the transmission of knowledge; and
- the criteria for evaluating students were multiple and diffuse.

The scheme of work used by the mathematics department looked incredibly sparse. Each academic year was split up into four or five topic areas. Within each area, the scheme of work gave a number of written objectives, a range of projects or investigations and a list of National Curriculum attainment targets. For example, in Year 9 the students were introduced to five topics: squares and cubes; connections and change; counting; geometry; and position and place. At departmental meetings, the teachers discussed the activities that they were about to use and any modifications they were intending to make, but there was little written documentation of the work. Some of the activities were written out on pieces of paper that were photocopied for the students; others were written up onto the board at the beginning of lessons.

The mathematics department had a relaxed approach to both the National Curriculum and the assessment of work. Their scheme of work was cross-referenced to the National Curriculum attainment targets but had no finer level of detail than this. When the teachers assessed the students' projects they wrote comments, describing what they considered to be good or bad about the work and ways in which students could improve the work. The teachers did not give grades and they did not keep records which they could pass on to teachers when the students changed groups. Most groups were taught by the same teacher as they moved up the school, unless a teacher left. The only other formative assessment the teachers made of the students took place when they walked around the room and interacted with students. The teachers at Phoenix Park tried to give a broad, holistic picture of students' achievement on particular projects. This stood in contrast to the marks or percentages which the Amber Hill students received for their answers to textbook questions.

At Phoenix Park, the teachers gave out projects and left students to develop them and use their own ideas. The teachers were available to help students but the students could not rely on this help as there was only one teacher in each room. Students were encouraged to work together and help each other as part of their work, and most students did this.

The students at Phoenix Park learned mathematics through the use of open-ended projects until January of Year 11. At this time, they started examination preparation. The projects were abandoned and students were introduced to formal methods and notations. The students were grouped according to the examination they were entered for: 'foundation', 'intermediate' or 'higher'.[2] The teachers used the blackboard more frequently to explain procedures and the students practised procedures within textbook questions, worksheets and past examination questions. The students reported that they found this system of learning mathematics very different from the one to which they had, by then, become accustomed.

Prior to joining Phoenix Park in Year 9, all the students had attended middle schools that used the SMP scheme. This meant that in Years 7 and 8, students at both schools had learned mathematics using the same SMP 11–16 booklets. In Year 9 the students in both schools then experienced a change in approach. At Amber Hill they moved to a more formal system of textbooks and class teaching. At Phoenix Park, the students abandoned set texts and moved to an extremely open, project-based approach.

The chapters that follow will describe the experiences of the students at the two schools in relation to these two approaches and the impact of these different school methods upon the students' development of mathematical understanding.

Notes

1 The mathematics National Curriculum, which all state schools in England and Wales must follow, is divided into five sections, called attainment targets. The first attainment target deals with mathematical processes, such as communication and reasoning.

2 The GCSE mathematics examination could, at the time of the research, be taken at one of three levels or 'tiers'. The three tiers gave access to different grades, with some overlap. Candidates taking the higher tier could attain a grade A*, A, B, C or fail; intermediate-tier candidates could attain a C, D, E or fail; and foundation-tier candidates could attain a D, E, F, G or fail.

4

Amber Hill mathematics: experiences and reflections

The first part of this chapter describes some important features of Amber Hill's approach to mathematics teaching. I have defined these features as important because they seemed to be the ones that had the greatest impact upon the perceptions and understandings that students formed. In the second part of the chapter I will represent the students' responses to, and ideas about, school mathematics.

The students' experiences

Structured questions

At Amber Hill the students worked from textbooks in each and every lesson in Years 9 to 11, apart from three weeks of Years 10 and 11 when they completed an open-ended coursework project. This meant that the vast majority of the students' experiences of mathematics involved short, procedural (Hiebert 1986) and closed questions. Some more open questions did feature at the end of exercises but when students encountered these questions, the teachers would normally close them down. Doyle asserts that teachers avoid classroom conflicts by 'redefining or simplifying task demands' and 'softening accountability to reduced risk' (Doyle 1988: 174). The Amber Hill teachers achieved this by breaking questions into small, atomistic parts and guiding students through any mathematical decision-making. Some teachers isolated the more demanding questions in the chapters and put them up on the board prior to lessons. In other lessons, teachers broke the problems down for students in one-to-one situations or with the whole class when a problem caused difficulty. They would generally do this using what Doyle and Carter (1984: 137) have referred to as 'extensive teacher prompting'. The teachers' motivation for this behaviour was clear – they wanted to help the students and to give them positive learning experiences. The following is a typical example, taken from my fieldnotes of a Year 9, set 5, lesson with Tim Langdon:

> Tim announces that he is going to put the 'problem' from the end of the chapter on the board. He draws:

Blagdon	0730	a	b
Westerfield	c	1045	d
Scaly Bridge	0845	1120	1535
Laughton	0935	e	f
New Harbour	g	h	1640

Tim then comes over to me and says: 'This is the classic problem with SMP, it gets them working down columns linearly or across and then suddenly there's a massive jump to this'. 'And they can't do it?' I ask. 'Well they can if you do this [*he strokes my arm*] and say "Come on you can do it, you can do it, do this bit and then do that bit"'. After Tim has put the problem on the board he gets all of the students to listen and then asks Gary, who Tim knows has worked out (f), to explain how he got his answer. Gary mumbles: 'You can see it takes one hour, no, 50 minutes to go from Scaly Bridge to Laughton so I done that, I added that onto Scaly Bridge and it come out 1625.' Whilst Gary is talking the other students look distracted and do not appear to be listening to him. Tim says: 'Good, which letter shall we work out next?' Tracey offers (e). 'Come on then Tracey,' says Tim. 'I'm not doing it,' Tracey says. Tim then asks: 'Well how long does it take to get from Scaly Bridge to Laughton?' 'No idea,' Tracey says. 'Come on, we've just heard how long!' Someone else calls out '50 minutes'. Tracey repeats this. 'OK,' says Tim, sounding exasperated, 'so what is 1120 plus 50 minutes?' 'Dunno,' says Tracey, then 'Oh, hold on, it's 1210'. 'See you can do it,' says Tim. 'Did I get it right?' Tracey asks with surprise. Tim says that she did. 'Oh cocker,' says Tracey, pleased.

Tim moves through the problem asking different students similar small questions each time. 'Well how long is it from here to here?' [*pointing to two times*] etc. Tim asks Michael to do one of the letters. Michael says: 'I can't do it.' So Tim leads him through it: 'How far did Leo say it was from here to here?' Michael trawls in his memory for the time, rather than trying to interpret the table. He gives the right answer. 'So how far is it from here to here?' Tim continues. Eventually Michael gets to the answer and Tim says: 'Wonderful, I thought you said you couldn't do it, have some confidence!' Tim continues with different students until all of the questions are completed. None of the students, even the last ones asked, attempt to get the answers without Tim leading them through the problem step by step.

(Year 9, set 5, Tim Langdon)

Thus, even in potentially open situations, the teachers created 'focused' environments (Walker and Adelman 1975: 47) for students. They combined high-definition questions which had one correct answer, with a closed sequencing of content, moving in 'tight, logical steps between one item and the next'. This is not unusual for teachers of mathematics. Schoenfeld (1988) and Doyle (1988) both claim that mathematics teachers commonly provide students with detailed structure in order to help them solve problems. Other research studies, such as Barnes *et al.* (1969), have also suggested that the tendency of mathematics teachers to ask closed questions with short factual answers which do not require any interpretation or reasoning, is not unusual.

In the most recent international survey (Beaton *et al.* 1996), teachers were asked whether they used questions involving reasoning in every mathematics lesson. England came 27th out of 38 countries in the proportion of teachers who said that they did (14%).

The predominance of the teachers' tendency to redefine questions and narrow their scope was not only evident in relation to questions which were open, but was also a more pervasive general tendency that seemed to form the basis of all mathematics instruction. In the majority of lessons I watched, the teachers would respond to the students' inability to answer questions by offering them a multiple-choice question, with one of two correct answers. For example, 'well, is it 4 or 5?' The students would select an answer, and if this was right, the teachers moved on. 'So is it the length or the width?' And so it proceeded. If students selected the wrong answer the teachers would repeat it, using a disbelieving tone, which was an indication that the students should plump for the other answer. The following extract is taken from a Year 11, set 3 lesson on trigonometry, taught by Hilary Neville:

> Hilary says: 'Yvonne, part b?' Yvonne says: 'Miss I can't do it.' Hilary responds saying: 'Well, what is DC to the angle; opposite or adjacent?' Someone calls out: 'Opposite.' Hilary continues: 'And we've just found B, which was what?' Someone offers: 'Adjacent.' Hilary continues: 'And opposite and adjacent give us what?' [*pointing to some trig ratios on the board*]. Someone offers: 'Tan.' Hilary asks: 'So tan what?' There is silence. So Hilary says: 'Tan 1.5.' Then: 'Tan 1.5 gives us what?' Someone puts this into their calculator and gives the answer: '14'. Hilary says 'correct' and moves on to the next question.
>
> (Year 11, set 3, Hilary Neville)

The teachers at Amber Hill rarely asked the students what they thought they needed to do, nor did they require them to place questions within a wider sphere of understanding. To help the students, they constructed paths that consisted of short, structured questions and these paths formed the basis of much of the mathematics guidance at Amber Hill. When students asked for help with their questions, the teachers did not talk to them about what they were doing. They would give them a series of instructions taking them through the questions:

> M: He says you do this to get that, you do this to get that and you go 'oh, right then'.
> H: Yeah, he gives you the answer, you write the answer down and that's it.
>
> (Maria and Helen, Amber Hill, Year 11, set 1)

The teachers broke problems down for students and gave them lots of help because they believed that this would give them mathematical confidence and, ultimately, help them learn mathematics. But the students and teachers seemed trapped within a vicious circle: the teachers thought that students would not or could not think; as a result, the students did not learn to think, and so the teachers' views were confirmed. In this way, the 'learned helplessness' (Diener and Dweck 1978: 451) of the students was continually reinforced. In interviews, the Amber Hill teachers seemed unaware of these tendencies. They reported that it was important for the students to find their own ways of solving problems. But in the harsh reality of the classroom, they did not allow this to happen. It was almost as if they were seduced into seeking and hearing correct answers. This seemed to be due to two important factors. First, they were concerned to get through as much work as possible and therefore did not have time to spend letting students grapple with problems:

> You're very stringent to a time limit, you haven't got the time, like, you couldn't spend, there's certain things you have to sit down and tell them. I could spend a week letting them work through on their own, or, I know this group, I could explain it to them in one lesson and they'd understand it, which one do you do?
>
> (Edward Losely)

Second, the teachers seemed to take this approach because they believed that students would experience failure if they did not structure work for them. The teachers were influenced in this regard, by the fact that most of the students were from working-class homes, a point to which I shall return later.

Standard mathematical methods

At Amber Hill, the mathematics teachers began lessons with a presentation from the board of the mathematical methods which students were intended to use in the exercises which followed. Teachers introduced students to the different procedures in a clear and structured way. However, they did not discuss their choice of mathematical methods, nor did they discuss with students when or why they worked. Students were not encouraged to discuss alternative approaches to problems or to try their own methods. Indeed many students reported in interviews that they were actively discouraged from using their own methods:

> JB: Do you get the impression in maths lessons that there is one method that you're meant to follow or do you get the impression that there are lots of methods that you could use?
>
> P: No, there's just one method, her method.
>
> D: In school you have to use the method you are told to do.
>
> (Paula and Danielle, Amber Hill, Year 10, set 2)

> Normally there's a set way of doing it and you have to do it that way. You can't work out your own way so that you can remember it.
>
> (Carly, Amber Hill, Year 11, set 1)

The teachers at Amber Hill were obviously keen to tell students about methods and strategies which were effective but they did not place these within a wider picture and they did not acknowledge the value of different or adapted approaches. The students' belief in the superiority of the teachers' methods meant that they endeavoured to learn these, even when their own methods held more meaning for them.

JB: Does the method that's given to you make sense to you?
J: Not as much as my own.
JB: Your own method makes more sense?
J: Yes.
JB: Why do you think that is?
J: I dunno, you . . . I dunno.

(Jackie, Amber Hill, Year 10, set 1)

The teachers' concern to impart standard procedures meant that when students asked for help with questions, teachers would reiterate the procedure they should be using, rather than discuss the meaning of the question. This was because the Amber Hill teachers regarded their major role in the classroom to be teaching the students mathematical methods, rules and procedures. They did not regard the teaching of procedures as *different* from the development of sense-making or understanding, and they did not perceive any need to teach anything other than their own standard or canonical methods.

The teachers' belief in the need to teach clear, standard methods also meant that they did not spend time linking different areas of mathematics or giving students an overall picture of the way different methods fitted into the mathematical domain.

JB: Does he talk to you about the way things are connected, do you talk about maths generally?
L: Not really, you just do bits, you just do one topic, then another.

(Lindsey, Amber Hill, Year 10, set 4)

One day or one week we're doing one thing and the next week we go onto a different topic.

(Anna, Amber Hill, Year 11, set 2)

Lessons generally involved a sequential presentation of disconnected topic areas which would be presented to students, one after the other, without any mention of any possible connections between them. The following notes were taken during a Year 10, set 4 lesson with Edward Losely:

The students all watch the board as Edward writes 'b = 30 BECAUSE THEY ARE ALTERNATE ANGLES'. Carlos shouts out: 'What does that mean sir?' Edward says: 'It means alternate.' He then announces: 'Right, we're going to move onto something else.' Daisy sighs and says: 'I need a break sir.' Edward ignores this and says, 'Textbooks out please, page 91, and writes <u>Metric Units</u> on the board.

Here Edward demonstrates his concern to move on to a new topic, which prevented him from explaining a term to Carlos. This sudden change in direction was not unusual. Amber Hill mathematics lessons derived their form from the artificial structure of a textbook which, inevitably, resulted in a somewhat disconnected presentation of mathematics. Hiebert and Carpenter (1992) suggest that connection-making in mathematics is central to the development of mathematical understanding and question whether students should be told about connections or given the opportunity to discover them themselves. Such issues did not form a part of the mathematics department's concerns at Amber Hill and students were not encouraged to do either of these things.

Within Bernstein's classification and framing analysis (Bernstein 1971: 57) Amber Hill's mathematics lessons would be ideally represented by 'collection codes'. Further, such a classification would be strong, rather than weak, on many counts. Importantly, the individual 'contents' of mathematics were well insulated from each other, but the lessons also conformed in terms of the explicit hierarchy which was established between teachers and students and the disconnection of lessons from everyday realities.

Rules to remember

In many instances, I noticed that teachers actively discouraged students from thinking about mathematical relationships by telling them rules that they should remember. This, again, placed Amber Hill's mathematics lessons within Bernstein's collection code (Bernstein 1971: 57) as, typically:

> 'There is a tendency . . . for the young to be socialised into assigned principles and routine operations and derivations. The evaluative system places an emphasis upon attaining states of knowledge rather than ways of knowing.

This describes the Amber Hill teachers' priorities well, because the teachers strove to give the students knowledge and they did not worry about 'ways of knowing'. The following extract is taken from my notes of a Year 11, set 3 class with Tim Langdon:

> Half way through the lesson Tim raises his voice above the low level of noise and tells everybody to listen. He then draws a figure on the board:

> 'If this is a line 3 long and 1 up what happens after a 90° rotation?' he asks. Some students shout out some answers. 'It goes round,' 'left,' 'right' are shouted out by three boys. Another boy makes a joke of this: 'It's up, down, left, right, north, south, east, west.' Tim tries again and hears another boy shout out: 'It goes up.' He responds: 'Yes, it does this doesn't it?' He then draws:

The students all look at the new drawing but do not respond. 'See what's happened?' Tim asks. 'They've swapped around, the 3 goes up and the 1 goes across, so remember, when you do a 90° rotation you just have to remember to swap them round.' All of the class listen to this instruction and then go back to their work.

(Year 9, set 1, Tim Langdon)

In this extract, Tim told the students to stop thinking about what happened during a rotation and remember a rule. The object of the SMP exercise was to get students thinking about the movements during rotations and to try them out for themselves. Tim discouraged the students from thinking about the movements, and gave them something to learn instead. The teachers gave the students these rules because they believed they would help them.

The simplification of mathematical principles or methods to a set of rules was common at Amber Hill. When Hilary taught trigonometry to her students she told them to learn the mnemonic SOHCAHTOA, as many teachers do, but she also gave the students other strict procedures that they should remember. The following extract is taken from my notes on one of Hilary's lessons on trigonometry, when the students are telling Hilary they do not understand:

A lot of the class are chatting now. Many of them are getting their questions wrong and seem to be very confused, so Hilary says: 'Look, Lindsey, if you have a problem with a right-angled triangle, what is the first thing you have to find?' This is a strange question and I am not sure of the answer to it, nor are the students. Sue tries: 'The angle?' Hilary says: 'So what do you do?' Sue offers 'sin?' Hilary obviously feels this isn't leading in the right direction and so starts again with: 'What is the first thing you've got to do with a right-angled triangle?' Someone suggests: 'Know the two sides?' Which seems to satisfy Hilary. She says: 'Yes, you've got to name them, you've got to know what the sides are.'

(Year 11, set 3, Hilary Neville)

In this part of the lesson Hilary tries to deal with the students' confusion by reducing the mathematical situation to a procedure the students should learn. The first part of this procedure was: 'When you see a right-angled triangle you label all the sides.' Students were intended to learn this so that they would label the sides of any right-angled triangles they saw, rather than interpret the particular situation they were placed in and decide what information they needed.

Hilary and the other teachers gave the students these 'handy hints' or rules to make mathematics questions easier, more straightforward, for students. The teachers understood the mathematics they were talking about and from that base of understanding the rules appeared to be helpful to them. But the students did not understand the rules they were learning or the way that these rules related to the different situations they encountered. They did not locate the rules within a broad mathematical framework and they did not develop a real sense of what they meant.

All of maths is just sums, rules and equations and none of it makes sense.

(Bridget, Amber Hill, Year 10, set 3)

I would suggest that this sort of mismatch between what the teachers and what the students gain from different rules underlies much of the confusion that students experience in secondary mathematics classrooms. Mathematics teachers understand what they are discussing and they often give students structured procedures to learn. These the teachers think will simplify and exemplify mathematical concepts. However, the students do not regard these procedures as particular ways of thinking about the problems or as examples of the methods in action. They view the procedures as abstract rules to be learned and to which they should adhere. Rules may be easy to learn, but difficult to use if they have not been placed within a wider sphere of understanding. Holt (1967) asserts that most teachers are driven by a desire to compartmentalize and provide models and structures that make sense for teachers but often do not for students. Mason (1989: 2–9) talks about a similar problem in relation to the exemplification of specific and unconnected instances. 'To the teacher they are examples of some good idea, technique, principle or theorem. To students they simply are. They are not examples until they reach examplehood.'

The teachers' motivations

The Amber Hill teachers were strongly motivated, with good intentions, to reduce the complexity of mathematical thought. This influenced their whole approach to mathematics teaching, causing them to close problems down, emphasize set methods and procedures, keep different topic areas distinct from each other and give students rules to remember. These approaches fitted in with the teachers' general philosophies about mathematics teaching, but there was evidence that the teachers had made their teaching *more* procedural and *more* rule-bound because of the social class composition of the school. Amber Hill was a largely working-class school and the teachers had low expectations for their students. In particular, they felt that the students had a reluctance to think for themselves or use their initiative:

> Students are generally good, unless a question is slightly different to what they are used to, or if they are asked to do something after a time lapse, if a question is written in words or if they are expected to answer in words. If you look at the question and tell them that it's basically asking them to multiply 86 by 32 or something, they can do it but otherwise they just look at the question and go blank.
>
> (Tim Langdon)

The different mathematics teachers shared the belief that the students were incapable of real thought but they did not relate this observation to the approach they offered at the school, but to the students themselves. In particular, features related to their background:

> I think there's a paucity of language here that the kids are using, that I think causes the problem. Having taught in Hertfordshire with much more breadth, with, if you like a professional background, there was higher performance there.
>
> (Tim Langdon)

I think the reading is a big problem with our children, they don't want to think about what they've read, then they'll say, 'I can't do it, I don't understand it,' and I think that's where it all breaks down as well. They have learned maths but they can't be bothered to think about it. It's got to do with ability and motivation as well, because in this school we have a lot of pupils who have very little motivation, you know? They're not encouraged at home.

(Leisel Harris)

I think textbooks are better for the pupils we've got, I think they get more advantage out of it. I think there's more motivation than – they don't need as high a motivation for a textbook than they do for individualized learning. And I think for the type of pupil we've got and parent, it's better that way.

(Hilary Neville)

The teachers' belief in the inadequacies of the students at the school made them think that a low-level structured approach would be most appropriate for them and this approach did not conflict with the teachers' views about good mathematics teaching. Anyon (1981) cites a number of studies (Leacock 1969; Keddie 1971; Sharp and Green 1975; Rosenbaum 1976) that have found that schools in poor and working-class areas 'discouraged personal assertiveness and intellectual inquisitiveness in students and assigned work that most often involved substantial amounts of rote activity' (Anyon 1981: 203). One of Anyon's studies found that mathematics teaching in working-class schools was procedural, rule-bound and involved the learning of set methods by rote. In more middle-class, professional and élite schools, the mathematics teaching involved choice, analytical reasoning, discussion of different methods and an emphasis upon mathematical processes (Anyon 1980). Amber Hill school conformed to this pattern and the teachers' approaches in the mathematics classroom seemed to derive partly from their views about the limitations provided by the students' home backgrounds.

The pace of lessons

In Years 9 to 11, the students were taught from the front of the class at a fixed pace, as is normal for setted classes (Dahllöf 1971). In the majority of cases, the pace of lessons was quite fast and all of the teachers demonstrated a concern to keep the students working through exercises quickly. This derived from a desire, on the part of the teachers, to complete as many SMP textbooks as possible, to cover all of the content they needed to cover and to satisfy the demands of the National Curriculum. This is not to say that the teachers adopted a markedly different practice prior to the National Curriculum; they probably did not. But the National Curriculum provided an extra time pressure and, in some senses, reinforced their view that teaching mathematics was all about covering a certain amount of content. This motivation to complete a large number of books seemed to mean everything to the teachers. In lessons and during conversations after lessons, the teachers spent a lot of time and energy worrying about the speed at which the class were completing books. Even when the teachers were explaining methods from the front of the class, they would often refer to the speed at which they were working, saying that they wanted to 'just quickly' demonstrate something. This was particularly prevalent in top-set classes. I took the following notes during a Year 9, set 1 lesson, taught by Tim Langdon:

> Tim arrives and immediately rubs some work off the board and says: 'OK, quadratic functions, we began, last lesson, very quickly, with $x^2 - 3x - 4$.' While he writes this on the board the class watch and listen in silence. 'And we said yesterday, how did we write this? Sara, you were the star yesterday.' Sara looks at him blankly. Tim says: 'Anyone?' They all look at him blankly. He moves on quickly saying: 'No-one knows? Well it was $(x + 1)(x - 4)$.' He writes this and continues. 'From the book yesterday, we were practising C1 yeah?, and C3?' Sara says: 'Sir we got stuck on [question] (e)'. Tim picks this up saying: 'Stuck on (e)? Well what number goes with x?' [the expression in question (e) is $x(x - 5)$]. Eventually someone says 'nothing'. Tim says: 'Yes, so the curve is $(x + 0)(x - 5)$, so nothing is nought, OK, C5, C6, so . . . C5a, what numbers will we get? Karina? [*silence*], Tafaz? What did you get?' Tafaz says: 'I didn't get nothing cause I didn't do it.' Tim continues: 'Well, what is the number?' Tafaz says: 'I dunno I can't do this chapter.' Tim moves on. 'Sara, what is the number?' Sara says: '4 and 3.' Tim comes back with: 'so what do they give you?' Sara says '12' and Tim starts to draw a curve on the board. All of the students are watching and listening in silence. So far, all of this lesson has been delivered at breakneck speed and I am not sure whether many of the students are understanding the concepts Tim is discussing. They can answer his small questions each time, such as 'What do 4 and 3 make?' but I don't know how much more than this they are understanding.
>
> (Year 10, set 1, Tim Langdon)

Part of the teachers' desire to move quickly through work meant that when they questioned students from the board, they did not waste time on students who could not provide correct answers. On numerous occasions I witnessed the different teachers speeding through demonstrations on the board and asking students questions, moving quickly around the class until they heard the right answers. The higher the set that the students were in, the more likely the students would be to get this fast and intense mathematical experience. These tendencies all created an impression that speed was very important in mathematics. Schoenfeld (1988) reports that this does not only put pressure upon students, it shapes their perceptions of what mathematical thinking involves. He found that students believed that mathematics questions should be answered within about two minutes – if they took any longer than this, they must have been doing the questions wrong. The implication is that mathematics involves working quickly, not thinking about things deeply (Schoenfeld 1988).

In Year 9, 163 students completed a questionnaire. This did not ask about the pace of lessons, but an open section asked the students to describe their mathematics lessons. This prompted 26 students (16 per cent) to say that lessons were 'too fast'. Typical comments from students were:

> We are pushed hard to get work done and we work constantly at a fast pace.

> The teacher rushes through methods faster than most pupils can cope.

The speed at which teachers took students through their work had an impact both upon the way students viewed mathematics as well as their learning of mathematics. Both of these responses will be considered now.

The students' reflections

Enjoyment

In all of my interviews with the 40 Amber Hill students, I received negative reports about mathematics lessons, even when students were chosen for interview because they had been reasonably positive about mathematics in questionnaire responses. This was not due to any prompting on my part. I generally started interviews with: 'Can you describe a typical maths lesson to me?' This was usually enough encouragement for the students to describe all of their negative feelings about mathematics. The reasons that the students gave for disliking mathematics, in interviews, were consistent with those given in questionnaires and classroom conversations. These related to the lack of variety in the school's approach, the lack of freedom or openness in the way that they worked and working as a class at a set pace.

Variety in lessons

The students at Amber Hill gave various indications that they were bored by their mathematical experiences. In their Year 9 questionnaire students were asked: 'What do you dislike about the way you do maths at school?'; 49 students (31 per cent) criticized the lack of variety in the school's approach and 77 students (48 per cent) reported that they would like more practical or activity-based work. Typical comments were:

> Maths would be more interesting if there were more projects to do.

> I don't think we should work on boring textbooks all the time.

> The way we always look at the same old textbooks (boring) and never change systems.

The students were dissatisfied, not only because they worked through textbooks for the vast majority of the time, but because they thought the questions within the books were very similar:

> S: The books are a bit boring, the chapters aren't really that good and they repeat the same questions over and over again, like when they explain something they do the question and then you have to do about twenty of them at the same time.

G: Yeah, and you only needed to do one, to know what's going on.
(Steven and George, Amber Hill, Year 10, set 3)

The students did not blame their boredom upon the intrinsic nature of mathematics. They were aware that they could gain enjoyment from learning mathematics, because they liked their coursework lessons and most of them had enjoyed their primary school mathematics. The students merely felt that it was inappropriate and unnecessary to work through SMP textbooks all of the time and they wanted more variety in their mathematics teaching:

JB: If you could change maths lessons what would you do?
R: I'd have maybe one lesson a week on the booklets, one on activities, one where you get a problem and you have to solve it – just a variety.
(Richard, Amber Hill, Year 11, set 2)

The students were far from unreasonable in their requests. In their Year 10 questionnaire the students were asked what they liked about mathematics lessons. The most popular response, given by 50 students (31 per cent), was: 'I like maths when we do activities'. Only four students (3 per cent) said that they liked their textbook work. When they were asked what they disliked about mathematics lessons, the four most common responses were: working from books (22 per cent), not understanding (20 per cent), work being all the same (19 per cent) and work being boring (17 per cent).

Open-ended work
In their textbook lessons, the students did not think that they were able to develop ideas, use their initiative or think about mathematics. They became aware of the value of these features of their learning when they were given open-ended coursework projects to work on for three weeks of Year 10. The students believed that the openness they experienced within coursework made mathematics more enjoyable, but also helped them to learn:

D: I feel restricted when we're doing the books.
R: Coursework is better than the bookwork you know, because with coursework you could go out and you can just – you learn more by doing something on your own, you know, if you're doing something on your own, you learn. Well I found I learned more by doing something on my own than I had done with the teacher.
(Richard and David, Amber Hill, Year 11, set 2)

S: It's a better way to learn.
JB: Why is that?
S: 'Cause I can figure it out for myself, the books just, it's too much leading you through it.
(Sacha, Amber Hill, Year 11, set 4)

The students described their coursework in terms of an increased cognitive demand. They did not regard coursework as an easy option and for many it meant a lot of effort and hard work, but they valued this experience because it allowed them to *think* and to feel ownership of their mathematics, in ways that textbooks never did:

L: It was a project, so it was going from one little thing and getting this big result at the end – working through on your own, going through different stages I was really proud of it actually, it was good.

S: We was dead chuffed weren't we?

L: You feel more proud of the projects when you done them yourself. If it's just working through the book, you can't feel proud – well, you can get them right and nobody cares – like you've seen it, it doesn't really matter, but if it's like a big project and you can see like what mark you've got at the end and if you've worked hard and if you get a good mark you feel really good about it.

(Lola and Sara, Amber Hill, Year 11, set 3)

The students felt a sense of ownership for their coursework projects, which they related to the amount of effort they had put into their work and the requirement to think about what they were doing. In the textbooks, the students were 'led through it', they were not allowed to 'work things out' and they felt 'restricted'. The students were clear that the openness of coursework enhanced their learning. Students were asked in their Year 9 questionnaire (before they had encountered coursework) to describe the 'most interesting piece of mathematics' they had ever done in a lesson and almost half of all students (49 per cent) cited the same mathematical experience – using 'LOGO' (a programming language) on the computer. When they completed a similar questionnaire in Year 10 and were asked to describe their favourite lesson, 62 per cent of students chose their 'open-ended tasks' and 9 per cent of students chose computer activities. A further 17 per cent either left the space blank, said that they could not name a good lesson or described something that was not related to mathematics, such as the teacher being away. Of the students who actually described a mathematical experience, 81 per cent chose their 'open-ended task' as their best ever mathematics lesson.

Working at their own pace

When the students began Year 9 at Amber Hill, they had just experienced two years of working through individualized booklets at their own pace. For many, the change from this system to a system whereby the whole class worked through pages of a textbook at the same speed was quite a shock. In interviews conducted in Years 10 and 11, working at the pace of the class was a major complaint for almost all of the students and one that they variously related to disaffection, boredom, anxiety and underachievement. Many of the students were unhappy because they felt that the pace of lessons was too fast. This often caused them to become anxious about work and to fall behind, which then caused them to become more anxious. This response was particularly prevalent amongst the top-set girls. However, the anxiety caused by fixed-pace lessons did not only prevail amongst the top-set students or girls. In the following extracts the students all relate the fixed pace of lessons to a loss of understanding:

A: I preferred the booklets.

S: Yeah, 'cause you just get on with it don't you?

A: Yeah, work at your own pace. You don't have to keep up with the others.

JB: Do you feel that now?

A: In a way, because if you don't do all the work, then you get left behind and you don't understand it.

(Anna and Suzy, Amber Hill, Year 11, set 2)

You don't learn it, you're just rushing and trying to make sure you get it done just so you don't get in trouble and you can catch up with every-one else.

(Lindsey, Amber Hill, Year 11, set 4)

The majority of students related their reservations about class teaching to what they perceived as a resultant loss of understanding. However, whilst some students, predominantly girls, complained about the fast pace of lessons, other students in the same groups said that their learning was diminished because lessons were too slow. These were usually boys:

M: It's silly now, it's just, most of the people slow the class down, gets it more boring.

C: You don't learn as much.

M: Like people laze around, when they've completed the work . . . say we've completed the work and we can go further up the book, we have to do that piece of work and then stop, and wait for the others to catch up and then people laze around.

(Marco and Chris, Amber Hill, Year 11, set 4)

The fact that some students complained about the pace of lessons being too fast, whilst other students in the same classes complained about lessons being too slow, seems to reveal an important limitation of a class-taught approach. For the teacher it shows how difficult it is teaching a group at the same pace, even when they are meant to be of 'homogeneous' ability. Amber Hill divided the students into eight sets which should produce relatively little variation amongst students in the same set, yet the students reported that the variation between them caused problems. The complaints of the different students at Amber Hill may also reflect the fact that the ability of a student does not necessarily indicate the pace at which they feel comfortable working, although this is an assumption upon which class teaching to setted groups is predicated. Further consideration of the implications of being in setted groups for the students at Amber Hill is given in Chapter 8.

Engagement

In the vast majority of lessons that I observed, students showed a marked degree of uninterest, uninvolvement and boredom with their work. Passivity was commonplace, demonstrated by rows of students quietly copying down methods without any apparent desire to challenge, question or think about their work. This was the way that the students responded to what they per-ceived as the boredom of lessons. In Corrigan's (1979) study of working-class

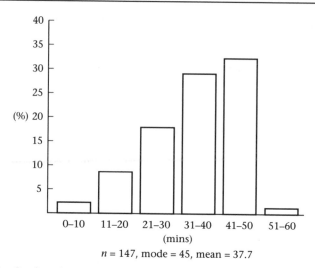

Figure 4.1   Students' perceptions of time spent working at Amber Hill

boys and their responses to schooling he found that 'mucking about' was a major activity in classrooms and not paying attention was endemic. Many of the Amber Hill students did not pay attention during substantial parts of lessons but they normally confined their 'mucking about' to quiet, non-mathematical conversations with friends. When I recorded the number of students working in lessons, over 90 per cent of students appeared to be on task at three different times, but when I asked all the students to write down, anonymously, how many minutes they worked in lessons, the average of all of the times given by the 147 students in the case study year group was 38 minutes (Figure 4.1).

The difference between my records of time on task and the students' perceptions of the time they spent working in lessons was partly due to the fact that students made sure that they looked as though they were working when they were not. It may also have been due to the fact that the students often worked through exercises they were given to do, without any thought or involvement:

> So we do equations and formulas, like roughly the same thing you do and you don't even like think about what you're doing, you just do it 'cause it has to be done.
>
> (Alan, Amber Hill, Year 11, set 3)

> As soon as you walk out the class . . . well actually as soon as the classroom starts, you don't really know anything, 'cause you've switched off. You walk in and you think, 'Oh another boring lesson' and you're off. As soon as you've walked out, you've forgotten about that lesson.
>
> (Keith, Amber Hill, Year 11, set 7)

The students often worked because they thought they had to, not because they enjoyed their work or because they were engaged with the mathematics. This meant that they were often working without thinking:

I think people start to think . . . 'Oh, I hate it, but we've got to do it, we haven't got much choice' . . . I think that's the thing that keeps people going on most of all. Like, if you asked people, 'Is maths your favourite subject?' hardly anyone would say it is, but they know they have to do it, 'cause it keeps getting drilled into them that you need maths, it's a good qualification. People think, 'Oh well, I've got to do it so I might as well do it.'

(Carly, Amber Hill, Year 11, set 1)

This attitude of 'I might as well do it' was not conducive to the students' learning and the students were aware that they could work in mathematics lessons without gaining very much from it:

Yeah, it depends if I'm in the mood, but I think, if it's like a lesson when I decide to work hard and I do work hard then I find that I succeed more, and I understand it more really, rather than if I just do it because I've got to do it.

(Maria, Amber Hill, Year 11, set 1)

Coursework was better because you could spend time on that and get involved with it, and you worked because you wanted to.

(David, Amber Hill, Year 11, set 2)

The difference the students highlighted between working when they wanted to work and working because they had to, is an important one. This is partly because this distinction may underlie the difference between learning and working procedurally. Almost all of the students talked about the time they spent in mathematics lessons 'switched off' and working without thought. In a sense, the Amber Hill students were exercising their own style of control over their work by not thinking – the only control that was open to them. This difference between learning and working without thought is also important because it raises questions about the validity and usefulness of time-on-task assessments (Peterson and Swing 1982). The students at Amber Hill would have looked to anybody as though they were hard at work, but their assessments of the time they spent working and their comments in interviews show that they spent much of their lessons with their minds elsewhere. The distinction the students drew between engaged and non-engaged work is also important because it suggests that the preoccupation teachers often have with keeping students quiet and orderly (Doyle and Carter 1984) may not be justified. The Amber Hill students said that they were engaged when they believed an activity to be worthwhile; at other times, they would 'work' but get very little out of it. This suggests that the nature of tasks that students are given to do is far more important than keeping them quiet and on task and 'high risk' tasks (Doyle and Carter 1984) that increase classroom disorder may ultimately be worthwhile.

Students' views about the nature of mathematics

Students at Amber Hill appeared to have developed very clear and consistent views about the nature of mathematics, the significance of which will emerge in later chapters. One important view, that was common amongst students, was that mathematics was a rule-bound subject.

Rule-following

Many of the Amber Hill students held a view that mathematics was all about memorizing a vast number of rules, formulas and equations. They did not believe that mathematics was a rich or varied subject, nor did they regard it as a 'doing discipline' (Treffers 1987: 60). They thought that their job in the mathematics classroom was to learn rules:

> At the end of each chapter if they had a list of rules it would be so much easier. Like now, I'm revising, I'm trying to go through the book and I'm looking for the rules. If they had the rules at the end it would be better . . . I bought a revision book from the school and they've got a few rules in it but again they sort of, you know, you've got to try and find the rules. They're not all set out for you.
>
> (Alan, Amber Hill, Year 11, set 3)

The students' belief in the need to remember rules had an important influence upon their mathematical behaviour. As a result of approximately 100 lesson observations at Amber Hill, I defined two main behaviours which seemed to influence the students' mathematical decision-making. One of these I termed 'rule following' because, when the students approached new situations, they did not try and interpret what to do; they tried to remember a rule they had learned. Part of the reason students did this was that they thought it was inappropriate to try and interpret the particular situation given to them, as there was only one specified way to solve each question and this involved remembering a rule:

> In maths, there's a certain formula to get to, say from a to b, and there's no other way to get to it, or maybe there is, but you've got to remember the formula, you've got to remember it.
>
> (Simon, Amber Hill, Year 11, set 7)

> In maths you have to remember, in other subjects you can think about it.
>
> (Lorna, Amber Hill, Year 11, set 1)

The students did not only believe that there were a lot of rules that could be learned in mathematics; they believed that they *had* to remember these rules in order to solve questions. Some of the students were so convinced of this, they did not see any place for thought within mathematics lessons. The predominance of the students' belief in the importance of remembering rules was further demonstrated by the Year 10 questionnaire which I devised in response to my fieldwork. In one item of this questionnaire, students were asked which they believed to be more important when approaching a problem: remembering similar work done before or thinking hard about the work at hand. Almost two-thirds of the students (64 per cent) said that remembering similar work done before was more important than thinking hard. This view appeared to be consistent with the strategies they employed in class and was, in many ways, indicative of their whole approach to mathematics. The Cognition and

Technology Group at Vanderbilt (1990: 3) note that when novices are introduced to concepts and theories they often regard them as new 'facts or mechanical procedures to be memorised'. The Amber Hill students rarely seemed to progress beyond this belief.

There were many negative consequences of the students' belief in the rule-bound nature of mathematics. One of these was that their desire to remember different rules meant that they did not try and interpret and understand what they were doing. Thus, they would learn rules and use them in situations to which they could easily be applied, but when the situations changed they became confused. A second negative consequence was that when students encountered questions that did not require an obvious and simplistic use of a rule or formula, many did not know what to do. In these situations they would give up on questions or ask the teacher for help. A third problem was provided for the students who thought that mathematics *should* be about understanding and sense-making (Lampert 1986). These students experienced a conflict at Amber Hill because they wanted to gain meaning and understanding but felt that this was incompatible with a procedural approach:

JB: Is maths more about understanding work or remembering it?
J: More understanding, if you understand it you're bound to remember it.
L: Yeah, but the way sir teaches, it's like he just wants us to remember it, when you don't really understand things.
JB: Do you find that it is presented to you as things you have got to remember, or is it presented to you as things you have got to work through and understand?
L: Got to be remembered.
J: Yeah, remember it – that's why we take it down in the back of our books see, he wants us to remember it.

(Jackie and Louise, Amber Hill, Year 10, set 1)

The students who wanted to understand their mathematics in depth were mainly girls. This will be discussed further in Chapter 9. These girls were in many ways more disadvantaged than the boys, most of whom were happy to just learn the rules and 'play the game'.

The students' belief in the need to follow rules caused problems for them because it had an enormous impact upon their behaviour. The students were confined by this belief and in new situations they did not try and think about what to do; instead they tried to remember a rule or method they had used in a situation they thought was similar. However, because in mathematics lessons they were not encouraged to discuss different rules and methods or think about why they may be useful in some situations and not others, the students did not know when situations were *mathematically* similar. This was part of the reason that they developed what I have termed cue-based behaviour (Schoenfeld 1985).

Cue-based behaviour

Frequently during lesson observations, I witnessed students basing their mathematical thinking on what they thought was expected of them, rather than on the mathematics within a question. Brousseau (1984) has talked about the 'didactical contract' (Brousseau 1984: 113), which causes students to base their mathematical thinking upon whatever they think the teacher wants them to do. I was often aware that the Amber Hill students used non-mathematical cues as indicators of the teacher's or the textbook's intentions. These sometimes related to the words of the teacher, but students would also use such cues as the expected difficulty of the question (what they thought should be demanded of them at a certain stage), the context of the question, or the teacher's intonation when talking to them. The following extract is taken from my fieldnotes of a Year 9, set 1 lesson:

> After a few minutes Nigel and Stephen start to complain because there is a question that 'is a science question, not a maths question'; they decide they cannot do it, and I go over to help them. According to the problem, 53 per cent of births are male babies and 47 per cent female babies, but there are more females in the population. Students are asked to explain this. I ask Stephen if he has any idea, and he says, 'because men die quicker' I say that this is right and leave them. Soon most of the students are putting their hands up and asking for help on the same question. Carol, a high-attaining girl, has already completed all of the exercise but has left this question out and says that she cannot do it.
>
> Later in the lesson, Helen has her hand up and I go over. The question says that '58.9 tonnes of iron ore has 6.7 tonnes of iron in it. What percentage of the ore is iron?' While I am reading this, Helen says: 'I'm just a bit thick really.' I ask Helen what she thinks she should do in the question, and she immediately tells me, correctly. When I tell her that she is right she says: 'But this is easier than the other questions we have been doing: in the others we have had to add things on and stuff first.' A few minutes later two more girls ask me for help on the same question: both of these girls have already completed more difficult questions.
>
> (Year 9, set 1, Edward Losely)

These two examples demonstrate different forms of cue-based behaviour. Nigel and Stephen and all of the other students who stopped working when they reached the question on babies stopped because the question required some non-mathematical thought. They could do the question, but they thought that their ideas must be wrong because they did not expect a question with 'science' in it in a mathematics lesson. The girls gave up on the question on iron ore because the mathematical demand was different from what they had expected. The previous exercise had presented a series of abstract calculations in which the students were asked to work out percentages that required them to 'add things on and stuff first'. In the next exercise the questions were mathematically simpler, but they were contextualized. The writers of the textbook obviously regarded these as more difficult, but the girls were thrown by this, because they expected something more mathematically demanding. This expectation caused them to give up on the question. It is this sort of behaviour that I have termed 'cue-based', because the students were using irrelevant aspects of the tasks, rather than mathematical sense-making or understanding, to cue them into the right method or procedure to use. Schoenfeld (1985) asserts that this sort of cue-based behaviour is formed in response to conventional pedagogic practices in mathematics that demonstrate specific routines that should be learned. This sort of behaviour, which was common amongst the Amber Hill students, meant that if a question seemed inappropriately easy or difficult, if it required some non-mathematical thought, or if it required an operation other than the one they had just learned about, many students would stop working.

The students used cues, such as implicit SMP rules, to help them know what to do in different situations. In a sense, the students were forced to do this because they had not learned to interpret situations or think about them mathematically. Their cue-based strategies were also effective; they often allowed them to attain correct answers. It was only in unusual situations, where the questions did not fit into the usual SMP prototype, that the students became confused. But these classroom strategies were ultimately destructive, because they worked against mathematical thinking. The methods discouraged sense-making and understanding and they were completely ineffective in non-SMP and non-classroom situations.

Summary

In this presentation of Amber Hill's teaching I have highlighted the closed, procedural, fast-paced and rule-bound nature of the students' experiences. I have not focused upon the friendly interactions between staff and students, the familar contexts teachers chose to illustrate ideas or the non-threatening aspects of their classrooms. I have chosen to focus upon more negative features of mathematics lessons, because these were central to the students' reports of their experiences and because these features seemed to be particularly influential in the development of students' understanding. However, although the combination of the characteristics I have chosen does present a fairly bleak picture, there are many indications in the literature that there was nothing unusual about Amber Hill's approach. Textbook teaching is employed by the vast majority of mathematics teachers (Romberg and Carpenter 1986). The UK's official body of mathematics inspectors reported in 1994 that most of the mathematics teaching they saw in the upper secondary years involved listening to the teacher and then working through exercises (Ofsted 1994: 5). Furthermore, Schoenfeld (1988: 163) asserts that textbook teaching generally entails the teaching of different content areas 'that have been chopped into small pieces which focus on the mastery of algorithmic procedures as isolated skills'. Doyle (1988) also reports that tasks which are based primarily upon memory, formulas and procedures are common in mathematics classrooms. The Amber Hill teachers were well-intentioned, committed and hard working. They kept the students on task, they prepared lessons well and they cared about their students. But they, like many other mathematics teachers, pursued the belief that students would learn and understand mathematics if they broke questions down and demonstrated procedures in a step-by-step fashion.

The students' responses to their textbook teaching at Amber Hill were consistent and fairly unanimous. Some of the students were content with their mathematics teaching and with the safety and structure of working through books every lesson, but the majority of students reported that they found this work boring and tedious. Most students preferred their coursework, partly because it was a change, but also because it gave them the opportunity to think about their work and use their initiative. The students valued this type of work because they felt that they gained understanding from it and this contrasted with what they felt they gained from textbook lessons. The students' behaviour when working through textbooks was consistent with these perceptions: they showed a marked degree of uninterest and uninvolvement, they reported 'switching off' as soon as lessons started and they worked procedurally without giving thought to what they were doing. The students wanted to understand more than they did and this was revealed by their preference for working at their own pace, which they felt gave them access to a deeper understanding. Not surprisingly, their fast, structured and uniform experiences of mathematics had clear and obvious consequences for the mathematical views they developed. The students regarded mathematics as a rule-bound subject and they thought that mathematical success rested on being able to remember and use rules. They thought that it was more important to remember similar work than to think about what to do and they rarely tried to interpret situations mathematically, because they had learned to recognise SMP cues and choose procedures and rules accordingly.

The structured and rule-bound nature of the school's mathematics approach seemed to have been exaggerated at Amber Hill because of the teachers' views about working-class students. The Amber Hill teachers would probably have taught mathematics in a closed, procedural way in any school, but they emphasized this approach at Amber Hill because they believed that the students found thinking and understanding particularly difficult. The students, in turn, were not confident or assertive with the teachers, and so they did not challenge this presentation of mathematics or question the teachers about the meaning of what they were doing. It was particularly ironic that for many of the students, their greatest wish was to be given the opportunity to think and use their initiative as part of their mathematics learning. In later chapters I will show the various ways in which the disciplined and structured nature of the students' mathematical experiences impacted upon their development of knowledge and understanding.

5

Phoenix Park mathematics: experiences and reflections

In a similar style to the last chapter, the two main parts of this chapter will describe some important features of Phoenix Park's approach and the students' responses to them.

The students' experiences

Open learning

Probably the most distinctive, influential and unusual aspect of the mathematics approach at Phoenix Park was its complete openness and the freedom that this created for students.

> In books, it tells you everything, you read everything off the question, you read the question and you have to answer it. Here you just have to make up your own, he just tells you what you have to do and then you have to do it yourself.
>
> (Gary, Phoenix Park, Year 10, JC)

> It was a big change from my last school, having the books and then just having it written on the board and being told to get on with it.
>
> (Andy, Phoenix Park, Year 11, RT)

The mathematical approach at Phoenix Park was open from the time when projects were described to students to the time, two or three weeks later, when they gave them in. This openness manifested itself in a number of ways: the way in which the projects were described and defined, the way in which teachers answered the students' questions and the way in which teachers guided students. The students at Phoenix Park were not given specified paths through their activities; they were merely introduced to starting questions or themes and expected to develop these into extended pieces of work. When they asked the teachers questions, the teachers seemed to make deliberate efforts not to structure the work for students:

> *JB:* When the teachers help you here, do they talk to you generally about the topic or do they break it down and tell you bit by bit what to do?

A: Very general, they hardly give you an answer.

D: Usually it helps, 'cause then they don't really give you the answer, you still have to work it out for yourself.

(Alex and Danny, Phoenix Park, Year 11, JC)

Thus the openness of the approach did not relate only to the way that mathematics was introduced; it also related to the way in which teachers interacted with students and supported them in their work:

Well, I think first of all you have to try and find your own methods; then if you really get stuck the teacher will come and give you suggestions for stuff and tell you how to – like – progress further and then you can kind of think about it.

(Andy, Phoenix Park, Year 11, RT)

I have chosen the following extract as a typical example of the way in which projects were introduced at Phoenix Park. In the extract, Jim Cresswell is introducing a new activity called '36 pieces of fencing' to a Year 9 class.

Twenty-five students come in and sit down. Sixteen boys and 9 girls gather around the board. A boy asks, 'Sir are we gonna start a new project?' Jim says: 'Yes, the title of the piece is 36 PIECES OF FENCING, [*he writes the title on the board*] so, you need a piece of paper — it only needs to be a scrap piece of paper at the moment, but make sure you've got something to write on.' A few get up and collect paper from a stand in the room. Jim continues: 'Can we have a bit of hush please? Right, you have a piece of fencing and from the side it looks like this:

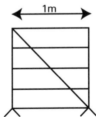

It has little legs on, like this and it is 1 metre wide. They have little hooks on and you can hook the gates together. You can put them at any angle, so those from the side would look like this:'

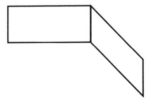

He continues: 'What we are interested in is what sort of shapes can you make with 36 pieces of fencing?' The students then start calling out shapes; a boy offers a square, a girl a hexagon. Someone asks: 'Do you have to use them all?' Jim says: 'Yes, there are rules,' and writes a heading RULES on the board and then, under this, USE THEM ALL ON EVERY SHAPE saying 'it makes them more manageable if you have to use them all.' Then, 'any other shapes?' A girl says 'rectangle'. Jim asks: 'Just one?' a boy says: 'A square is a rectangle' and Jim says 'Yes, we've already got a special type of rectangle.' The students continue shouting out shapes, a boy says 'rhombus' a girl says 'parallelogram' and Jim is adding all of these to a list on the board; another boy says 'pentagon' and Jim stops at this and says 'Can you?' The boy says 'yeah'. Jim asks 'How many sides?' and a few offer 'five'. A girl says 'You've got 36 fences' and Jim says 'Well you can have a pentagon, but what will it be like?' There is silence, so he asks: 'Will the sides be the same?' The students all shout 'no'. Jim asks, 'So what will it be called?' A boy offers 'irregular'. Jim writes IRREGULAR PENTAGON then asks for more shapes. One boy suggests a quadrilateral and Jim says 'Yes, well, these are all quadrilaterals' and he points to some shape names. He puts brackets round these on the board and writes QUADRILATERALS next to them. He then continues with, 'We've got a triangle but is there only one?' A girl says, 'There's loads.' Jim says: 'Yes there's loads so lets put an s on' and makes it triangles, then 'so, we've got four sided, five sided ...' A boy offers 'octagon' and a girl says 'Yes, eight sides'. Jim asks: 'Yes, but what will happen?' Someone says, 'There'll be some left over' and Jim says 'Yes, or irregular, not all the same length, so 'pentagon' and writes (IRREGULAR) HEPTAGON (IRREGULAR) OCTAGON (IRREGULAR)' A boy offers 'nonagon' and Jim tells him to say it louder so that everyone can hear. Jim writes it on the board with '(9)' next to it, then asks 'Will it be regular or irregular?' A girl says 'regular' and Jim asks why. She says, 'cause nines go into 36.' Jim asks 'What other regular ones can we have?' There is silence and he adds, 'Well, the definition seems to be if the number of sides go into the number of fences'. A boy says '12' and Jim writes DODECAGON (12 SIDED), someone offers '18' and Jim says he doesn't know what that is called but writes up 18-SIDED SHAPE. A boy says 'three sides' and someone else says, 'That's a triangle.' Jim asks: 'OK how many regular triangles can you make?' Someone says, 'One' and Jim says, 'Yes, where I've written regular you can also have irregular ones.' He then asks, 'Which are easier to draw?' Someone says 'Irregular' and Jim says, 'OK shall I make it harder and say we only want regular ones?' Some say 'no' to this and some say 'yes'. Jim says, 'We can put another rule in if you want' and writes under the rules heading ONLY MAKE REGULAR SHAPES but then adds (YOU CAN BREAK IT SOMETIMES). Justin says, 'I always break the rules sir' and Jim says 'Really, Justin'. Then, 'Now, tell me something about a square.' A girl says, 'They're all the same length.' Jim says, 'Yes so I have to go round four lengths all the same and if I call this *m*.' He draws:

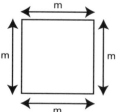

and says, 'I'll say four times *m* equals what?' A girl and boy say '36' and Jim asks 'So how do I work out what *m* is?' A few say nine, one girl says '36 divided by 4,' Jim responds to these saying, 'There are two ways of looking at it, we can say $4 \times m = 36$ by thinking about our times table, or we can say $36 \div$ by $4 = m$, but you can only really use the first when it's a whole number.' Then, 'So how big is it? What is the area?' A few say '81' and Jim says, 'So the area is 81 metres squared. Why metres squared? Because it's an area, when you work out area it's metres squared.' Then, 'I want you to look at all of those shapes and find ones that are possible to do, and I'm interested in the area of them. Why might I be interested in area? What is it useful for? I may be making a garden, or a pen.' Jim suddenly turns to a boy near him who has been chatting incessantly and says, 'Michael, it is irritating you talking all the time, OK?' Michael looks repentant and Jim continues: 'So I'm interested in area, I'd like you to explore these shapes and find areas. Now, the first thing I'd like you to do is record what I've been talking about; my writing isn't sufficient, you need to put things in your own words, your version of the problem, expand it, write what it means, pick out shapes, decide what order you need to do them in!' As the class go back to their seats and start work, Matt, who is new to the school, says 'Sir, I don't understand these shapes, I don't think I've seen them before.' Jim says, 'Well that could be one of your tasks. Find out about the shapes, look them up in your maths dictionary, or you could look in an ordinary dictionary.'

Most of the class start work. Some are talking. Some have started straight in with drawing squares. Some check with Jim what they are meant to be doing. Two boys sitting at the back are talking about something else and not working. Matt is looking up the shapes in a dictionary. Most students seem to have started doing the task, without explaining in their own words what they have to do, as Jim suggested. Three boys sitting together at the back are slow to get started, they write a few words, talk for a while, write some more and so on. Two boys pick up their table and move it round to avoid the sun. Jim is kneeling down by the side of somebody saying, 'You draw it whatever size you want to draw it.' Most of the students' introductions say, 'We need to see how many shapes we can make out of 36 fences' or something similar. Four girls are sitting having an animated and excited conversation about what all of the different shapes are: 'Is it a quadrilateral?' [*laughs*] another 'What's that?' Another '– a trapezium?' They seem very interested. As I pass Julie she checks with me what a regular shape is before she writes out her definition in her introduction. Some students have now written about a paragraph. Three boys at the back have only written a heading and a sentence; most of the rest of the class have moved onto examples. None of these students is using a calculator, nor do they ask for them, although they are available. One of the boys is finding out which is bigger, a rectangular area or a triangular area. Jim comes over and says, 'So which was bigger?' The boy tells him and he asks, 'Is that what you would think, does it look bigger?' They discuss this for a while.

(Year 9, Jim Cresswell)

The extract above is a fairly typical example of an introduction to a project on which the students worked for approximately three weeks. The only slightly unusual aspect was that the students were given one project to work on, rather than a choice of projects. Jim's introduction incorporated a number of features which related to the openness of the approach. Jim introduced the problem of '36 fences' by getting the students to think about the different shapes that were possible. He did not spend much of the time at the board telling the students information, rather he created an arena for discussion and negotiation. During the course of this discussion, the students encountered the need for certain parameters, such as 36 fences must always be used and irregular shapes are not allowed. Jim did not tell the students these constraints at the beginning but waited for them to be raised by the students. At the end of the class discussion, Jim told the students that it was not enough to write the problem out in his words, they needed to reformulate it in their own words, using their own thoughts. Importantly, Jim did not give them any particular question to answer, he just said, 'I am interested in area, I'd like you to explore these shapes and find areas.' When Matt said that he was not familiar with the shapes, Jim suggested a place that he could find out about them; he refrained from telling Matt what he needed to know. When the students started their work, Jim left them to their own devices. He did not 'police' the room or check that they were going about things in a specific way. When he could, he interacted with students and engaged them in conversations about their work. When one of the students said that a triangular area was bigger than a rectangular area, Jim did not focus upon the answer; he asked him whether he would expect this, whether it looked bigger – he encouraged him to think about the situation.

It was also typical that students did differing amounts of work in the remainder of the lesson. Some copied Jim's introduction or another student's introduction in a fairly absent-minded way and did nothing else. Some started their work in a relaxed way, interspersing it with non-mathematical conversations; others engaged in lively debates about the problem. These varying responses to the task were allowed to develop undisturbed and Jim did not attempt to change anything the students were doing, or not doing. By the end of the first lesson, the students had produced very different amounts of work which focused upon different questions and problems. As time went by and more lessons were spent on the theme, the students began to diverge more and more, both in the amount of work they did and the topics they worked on.

Teachers introduced activities to students which they knew were mathematically rich, but the teachers did not have fixed ideas about the ways in which students would interact with the problems. In a Year 11 lesson taught by Martin Collins, Shelley was working on an investigation called 'Discs'. She started off working with four discs (or numbers) and then moved onto five:

After working on the problem for a while, Shelley takes it over to Martin to show him. He looks at the work, laughs and says, 'Golly, I didn't know it could get that complicated.' Shelley says, 'Shall I stop?' Martin says, 'No, carry on.' Shelley says, 'I want to carry on because I want to see what happens to the horizontals when I continue up in this direction.'

(Year 11, Martin Collins)

This extract is interesting, not because Shelley was extending the activity in an unusual or idiosyncratic way, but because Martin had obviously not encountered the work before. Shelley also demonstrated in this extract that it was the unknown aspect of the exploration that held her interest. She was genuinely interested to know what the mathematical outcome would be of extending the work. When students showed the teachers their work, they did not seem to expect the teachers to have seen it before. They did not expect them to look and say, 'Yes that is right' but to look and see whether they were moving in an interesting direction. Such interactions then formed the basis for dialogue between the students and teachers.

The students at Phoenix Park gave many indications that they eventually formed their expectations and ideas about learning mathematics in relation to an open approach. This was demonstrated clearly by a lesson in which Tony Garrett, a student teacher attempted to teach the students in a more traditional and closed way:

> Tony starts the lesson by asking the class to copy what he is writing off the board. He is writing about different forms of data, qualitative and quantitative. The students are very quiet and they start to copy off the board. Tony then stops writing for a while and tells the students about the different types of data. He then asks them to continue copying off the board. After a few minutes of silent copying, Gary shouts out: 'Sir when are we going to do some work?' Leigh follows this up with: 'Yeah are we going to do any work today sir?' Barry then adds: 'This is boring, it's just copying.' Tony ignores this and carries on writing and talking about data. The boys go back to copying. Tony asks Lorraine if she is 'OK'. She says: 'No not really, what does all this stuff mean?' Tony ignores this and goes back to writing on the board. Gary persists with his questioning, this time asking: 'Sir, why are we doing all this?' Tony says: 'We are just rounding off the work you have done.'
>
> After about 20 minutes of board work, Tony asks the students to go through all of their examples of data collection that they have done over recent weeks and write down whether they are qualitative or quantitative. Peter asks: 'Sir, what's the point of this, aren't we going to do any work today?' Tony responds with: 'You need to know what these words mean.' Peter replies: 'But we know what they mean, you've just written it on the board so we know.'
>
> (Year 10, Tony Garrett, student teacher)

This series of interactions is particularly interesting because the group of students continually resisted the work Tony was doing with them because they simply did not regard it as work. A group of boys repeatedly asked, '[are we] going to do any work today?,' indicating that they did not regard copying as work, probably because it did not require any thinking or present them with a problem to solve. When Tony told them to classify data as quantitative or qualitative so that they would learn what the words meant, Peter questioned the point of this because they had already been told what they meant. Yet the mathematics offered in this example is fairly typical of a standard secondary school mathematics lesson in which the teacher explains what something means to students on the board, they copy it down and then they practise some examples of their own. The degree of resistance the students provided to this work seems to indicate that they found the approach alien. In another of Jim Cresswell's lessons, one of the students complained to Jim about being away last lesson saying, 'It was terrible; we had this teacher who acted like he knew all the answers and we just had to find them.'

The students gave other indications that they regarded their mathematics learning as an open experience. In interviews in Year 10, I asked the students to say whether they thought mathematics lessons were similar to any other lessons at the school. Sixteen of the 20 students said that mathematics was most similar to art, English or humanities; nobody compared mathematics to the subjects more traditionally linked to it, such as science.

JB: Is maths similar to any other lessons at Phoenix Park, or is it different?

L: I suppose it's a bit like English and art and stuff, English, when you're left to do your own work – they explain at the beginning what to do and then you're left on your own to do it.

(Lindsey, Phoenix Park, Year 11, JC)

Time on task

A second striking aspect of school mathematics at Phoenix Park related to the number of students who were 'off task' in lessons, which continued to be a source of surprise to me. In their Year 10 questionnaire, students were asked to describe their mathematics lessons to someone from another school. The most popular description from 23 per cent of students was 'noisy'. In the 90 or so lessons I observed at Phoenix Park, I would typically see approximately one-third of students wandering around the room, chatting about non-work issues and generally not attending to the project they had been given. In some lessons, and for some parts of lessons, the numbers 'off task' would be greater than this. Some students remained off task for long periods of time, sometimes all of the lessons; other students drifted on and off task at various points in the lessons. In a small quantitative assessment of time on task I stood at the back of lessons and counted the number of students who appeared to be working ten minutes into the lesson, half way through the lesson and ten minutes before the end of the lesson. Over 11 lessons with approximately 28 students in each, 69 per cent, 64 per cent and 58 per cent of students were 'on task', respectively.

The freedom that the students experienced to stop working when they wanted to seemed to be created by a number of interrelated facets of the Phoenix Park approach. It was partly to do with the nature of the mathematics approach and the fact that students could be wandering around the room and chatting with other students as part of their work. It also related to the fact that the students could all have been working on something different which made it difficult for teachers to monitor the amount of work that they did:

T: It gives some people more of a chance to muck about.

JB: Why?

T: Because, for instance, at the end of a lesson if the teacher wanted to check how much work you'd done he couldn't, but if you started at number 1 he would know that you hadn't got to number 20 or whatever.

(Trevor, Phoenix Park , Year 11, RT)

More important than either of these factors however, the freedom the students experienced seemed to relate directly to the relaxed and non-disciplinarian nature of the three teachers and the school as a whole. Most of the time the teachers did not seem to notice when students stopped working unless they became very disruptive. All three teachers seemed concerned to help and support students and, consequently, spent almost all of their time helping students who wanted help, leaving the others to their own devices. The three teachers were not markedly different in this regard, although Jim Cresswell's lessons were noticeably more chaotic than those of the other two teachers.

> I think the weakness of my teaching style would be very much that I depend on willingness and co-operation and, you know, if somebody is motivated to do the stuff they will achieve well.

(Jim Cresswell)

Jim often told me that he was 'no good at discipline' and my lesson observations showed that students in his classes were less 'on task' than the classes of other teachers. This seemed partly to be because he treated the students in a very adult way which some of the students took advantage of. For example, there was a small classroom attached to Jim's room that nobody used. Jim used this room as a 'talking room' and students were meant to work in there if they wanted to talk and work, leaving the other students to work in quieter conditions. Jim was not concerned about his inability to see the students in this room and he rarely asked students to work when they were not doing so, unless they became disruptive. When Jim did tell students to work, the result was often ineffective. Typically, the students would say something back to Jim which sparked a debate between Jim and the student. At the end of this the student usually went back to not working and Jim would usually be called away to help somebody. In a number of Jim's lessons I observed, so few of the students appeared to be working that I started to have serious doubts about my research. At the end of my research I found out that some of the newer, more middle-class parents at the school had complained about Jim's teaching which resulted in the head teacher visiting his lessons and telling Jim that only about 30 per cent of students were on task.

Both Rosie Thomas and Martin Collins showed more overt concern to keep students on task than Jim. But whilst both teachers were more likely to react to the extremes of behaviour that Jim tolerated, they nevertheless seemed unconcerned about students who sat and chatted through most of their mathematics lessons. When the two teachers did ask students to work, this often had little effect: the students worked for a few minutes then went back to chatting. The degree to which students were on task in lessons also varied between classes, year groups and aspects of lessons. In later sections I will explore the impact of the independence that students experienced over their workrate, which produced some surprising results.

Independence and choice

There were many overt and covert ways in which the students at Phoenix Park were encouraged to be independent. This meant that they needed to take on some responsibilities as part of their mathematics approach in order to succeed. For example, the students were not given exercise books for their work: they used pieces of paper. At the start of activities they were given blank or lined pieces of A4 paper as well as graph paper if they needed it. The students each had a box file in which they kept their work. Nobody took charge of this process for the students, papers were not collected in at the end of lessons. Students were meant to either take them home and bring them back again or store them in their box file. Students often came to lessons having forgotten or lost their work from the previous lesson and so took a new piece of paper and continued on that. Some of the students were very disorganized and their box files were made up of odd collections of extracts from different activities. At the end of each project, students were meant to gather together all of their work, present it in a coherent fashion and summarize it. The students were rarely encouraged to be careful or tidy and many of the finished projects looked very messy in comparison with a more typical mathematics exercise book.

At around Easter of Year 11, the school sent pieces of course work to the examination board. At this time the students were told to choose their best two pieces and give them in. The choice of course work was left up to the students, although the teachers would give guidance if asked. Often the pieces of course work which were sent to the board were unfinished, either because the students showed little concern for the task of choosing their course work or because the students had no complete projects to send:

> L: They left it to the last minute as well, like they kept saying you've got to have work for your GCSE and that, but if you didn't hand your projects in, in Years 9 and 10 they weren't really bothered, were they?
> H: No.
> L: And at the end now they say we need them.
> (Louise and Hannah, Phoenix Park, Year 11, JC)

Here the students relate the incompleteness of their work to the lack of enforced discipline or control from their teachers. Another important aspect of the mathematics approach which required the students to take responsibility for their work involved the choice that students were given about the projects they could work on and the direction the students took their work in. The students at Phoenix Park were given considerable and varying amounts of freedom in their choice of work, their approach to work, the way in which they behaved in lessons, the organization of their work and even their work environment.

The amount you do is always up to you isn't it? How much homework you do and especially course work for GCSE, it's your work, it's your responsibility. I mean however much work you get in, that's always going to be reflected in your mark.

(Nile, Phoenix Park, Year 11, JC)

This choice and the students' independence had an important impact upon their responses to mathematics, which will be considered now.

The students' responses

Enjoyment

In interviews, conversations and lesson observations at Phoenix Park the students gave a much more varied picture of their enjoyment than the students at Amber Hill. Whereas the Amber Hill approach prompted a fairly consistent reaction from the students, the Phoenix Park approach seemed to divide the year group into those who loved it, liked it and hated it.

Approximately half of the cohort at Phoenix Park liked mathematics most of the time, but their enjoyment depended upon the particular projects they were working on. Approximately one-third of the students were more positive than this and they seemed to like everything about mathematics. Questionnaires and interviews in Years 9 to 11 showed that these students liked the approach because it was varied, because they were given a choice about what they did and because they had the freedom to work in any direction.

V: I thought the activities were really interesting because you had to work out for yourself what was going on, you had to use your own ideas.

JB: How does that compare to the SMP work you used to do in middle school?

V: Boring, it was boring doing stuff out of books.

(Vicky, Phoenix Park, Year 11, JC)

You're able to explore more, there's not many limits and that's more interesting.

(Simon, Phoenix Park, Year 11, JC)

However this freedom was also the reason that the third group of students 'hated' the approach. These students thought that mathematics was too open and they did not want to be left to make their own decisions about their work. They complained that they were often left on their own not knowing what to do and they wanted more help and structure from their teachers. The students felt that the school's approach placed too great a demand upon them – they did not want to have to use their own ideas or structure their own work and they said that they would have preferred to work from books. What for some students meant freedom and opportunity, for others meant insecurity and hard work.

You don't mess about if you've got a book there, you know what to do.
(Megan, Phoenix Park, Year 10, RT)

There were approximately five students in each class who disliked and resisted the open nature of their work. These students were mainly boys and they were often disruptive, not only in mathematics but across the school.

In the Year 9 questionnaire item which asked students to describe the 'most interesting piece of mathematics' they had ever done in a lesson, the Phoenix Park students responded in a very different way from the Amber Hill students. Whereas 49 per cent of Amber Hill students chose 'Logo', Phoenix Park students described a variety of different projects. Five different projects were nominated by at least 5 per cent of students: 11 per cent of students chose 'Logo', 10 per cent an activity called 'Frogs', 9 per cent a probability project, 8 per cent chose the 'maths day' (when they worked on mathematics projects all day) and 6 per cent chose an activity called 'Limping seagulls'. Another 36 per cent of students chose other class projects which they had encountered over the past year. The question asked students to describe the most interesting piece of mathematics they had ever done in a school lesson. Many of the Amber Hill students described a lesson from primary school or from Years 7 and 8. At Phoenix Park, all of the students described one of the projects they had experienced since starting at Phoenix Park in Year 9 and all descriptions were positive, for example:

Horse racing was good because the answers were unexpected.

The best piece of maths I think I have done was boxes as I did quite a long project.

Statistics. I thought this was the most interesting. I wrote a large amount about marriages and divorces using the book *Social Trends*.

The Phoenix Park students' replies gave the impression that they were genuinely interested in the projects that they had chosen and they did not report that mathematics lessons were monotonous or boring.

In Year 9, students from both schools were asked in a questionnaire to state how often they enjoyed the mathematics they did in school ('always', 'most of the time', 'sometimes', 'hardly ever' or 'never'). This closed question produced similar results from the two schools. Forty-three per cent of Amber Hill students and 52 per cent of Phoenix Park students reported enjoying mathematics 'always' or 'most of the time'. However, the students responded very differently to open questions on the same questionnaire, indicating that the closed questions may have been less effective at eliciting the students' real feelings. One question asked the students to describe what they disliked about mathematics at school and 44 per cent of Amber Hill students criticized the mathematics approach and 64 per cent of these students criticized the textbook system. At Phoenix Park, 14 per cent of students criticized the school's approach and the most common response, from 23 per cent of students, was to list nothing they disliked about mathematics at school; this compared with 6 per cent of Amber Hill students. Table 5.1 presents all of the responses the students gave to the three different open questions on the questionnaire

Table 5.1 Year 9 open questionnaire responses (per cent)

Nature of comment	Amber Hill (n = 382)	Phoenix Park (n = 202)
Enjoy open-ended work	14	38
Dislike textbook work	22	0
Cannot understand work	20	6
Can understand work	3	5
Work is interesting	4	21
Want more interesting work	15	19
Want more group work	5	0
Enjoy working alone/with others	8	4
Pace is too fast	9	3
Pace is about right	0	3

which asked students what they liked, disliked and would like to change about mathematics lessons. These three questions prompted 382 comments from the 160 Amber Hill students and 202 comments from the 103 Phoenix Park students (there were no significant differences between the number of comments per student at the two schools). The responses have been combined in order to present an overview of the issues important to the students. One of the most obvious differences which is demonstrated by these results is that when students were invited to give their own opinions about mathematics lessons, the Phoenix Park students chose to comment upon the interest of their lessons and their enjoyment of open-ended work, whereas the Amber Hill students were more concerned about lack of understanding and their dislike of textbooks. Many more of the Amber Hill students would probably have talked about open-ended work if they had ever experienced any, but at that time they had not yet worked on their course-work projects. In response to the three questions above, there were a total of 88 comments from Amber Hill students about their perceived lack of understanding of mathematics, compared with six comments from the Phoenix Park students.

In their Year 10 questionnaire the students from both schools were asked to write a sentence describing their mathematics lessons. The three most popular descriptions from the 75 respondents at Phoenix Park were 'noisy' (23 per cent), 'a good atmosphere' (17 per cent) and 'interesting' (15 per cent). This contrasted with the three most popular responses from the 163 Amber Hill respondents which were 'difficult' (40 per cent), something related to their teacher (36 per cent) and 'boring' (28 per cent). The students' sentences were also coded as either: very positive, positive, neutral, negative or very negative. Table 5.2 shows the distribution of results for the two schools.

The overall picture of enjoyment gained from Phoenix Park was therefore more varied and significantly more positive than that gained from Amber Hill. I have not discussed the aspects of mathematics that the Phoenix Park students disliked in the detail that I discussed the dissatisfaction of the Amber Hill students. This is because the Phoenix Park students expressed considerably less concern about their school's approach and there was not a similar

Table 5.2 Describe maths lessons: coded questionnaire responses (per cent). For Amber Hill, $n = 154$; for Phoenix Park, $n = 67$

School	Very positive	Positive	Neutral	Negative	Very negative
Amber Hill	0	23	38	33	6
Phoenix Park	5	38	32	25	0

consensus of opinion about its reported inadequacies. A consideration of the various forms of data, including questionnaires, interviews and lesson observations suggests that approximately one-third of the Phoenix Park students positively liked mathematics, particularly because of its variety and openness, approximately one-half of students enjoyed some of the projects some of the time and disliked others at other times and the remaining students disliked the approach, particularly the freedom and openness they experienced. I will consider this last group of students in more depth in a later part of this chapter.

Engagement

The general picture

The students at Phoenix Park varied in the extent to which they engaged with their mathematics. The students were essentially left to decide whether or not they worked in class. This meant that some students worked with enthusiasm on their mathematics projects, whilst others would find talking or disrupting the class more interesting than their work. It was difficult for the students to work in a 'switched-off' procedural way at Phoenix Park because the students constantly needed to take decisions about their project work. This meant that students tended to be either interested and working or uninterested and not working. The following extract is taken from the third lesson on the theme '36 fences' which was described earlier, taught by Martin Collins. Some of the students have considered the areas of different rectangles with a perimeter of 36, others have moved on from this and have started to investigate the areas of different shapes:

> Mickey has found that the biggest area for a rectangle with perimeter 36 is 9×9 and is moving on to find the area of equilateral triangles, compared with other triangles; he seems very interested by his work. He finds one area and is about to find another when he is distracted by Ahmed who tells him to forget triangles, he has found that the biggest possible shape made of 36 fences has 36 sides. He tells Mickey to find the area of a 36-sided shape too and leans across the table explaining how to do this excitedly. He explains that you divide the 36-sided shape into triangles and all of the triangles must have a 1-cm base. Mickey joins in saying, 'Yes and their angles must be 10 degrees!' Ahmed says, 'Yes but you have to find the height and to do that you need the tan button on your calculator,

T-A-N, I'll show you how, Mr Collins has just shown me.' Mickey and Ahmed move closer together to do this.

On another table I ask Clare what she is doing, she says that she is working out the area of a hexagon and she shows me her diagram. She explains that she is working out the area by dividing it into six triangles, she has drawn one of the triangles separately. She says that she knows that the angle at the top must be 60° so she can draw it exactly to scale using compasses and find the area by measuring the height. Clare seems to have made these decisions on her own and she is clearly interested in her work. On another table, six girls have not started work even though we are 20 minutes into the lesson; they are sitting colouring on their folders; another group of boys is working out the areas of rectangles but they do not seem to be particularly interested in what they are doing.

(Year 9, Martin Collins)

This extract demonstrates the different amounts of enthusiasm and interest that were commonly in evidence during Phoenix Park lessons. Mickey and Ahmed were two high-attaining boys who were extremely involved in their work and who seemed genuinely excited to be discovering some new information. The interest they showed for trigonometry, because they could *use* a tangent ratio to help them find something out within their project, was vastly different from the interest the Amber Hill students showed towards trigonometry. Clare was not a high-ability student but she was also interested in what she was doing and the decisions she had made. The six girls who were drawing on their folders were clearly not interested at all and the small group of boys working out the areas of rectangles were not working with enthusiasm.

An important difference between Amber Hill and Phoenix Park was that Phoenix Park students were not made to work. In interviews the students did not talk about work that they had done because they had been forced to, but had gained little from in the way that the Amber Hill students did. They talked instead about the choice they had between involvement and doing nothing:

It was definitely a lighter lesson – you'd be involved and if you didn't want to be involved you'd sort of sit back and watch it all happen I suppose.

(Hannah, Phoenix Park, Year 11, JC)

Here Hannah does not give working without involvement as an option, whereas this was something of which the Amber Hill students were very aware. Hence, although the freedom that the students at Phoenix Park experienced over their work rate meant that some students did very little, it also meant that some students worked in a very motivated way. When students were asked to say the amount of time they worked in lessons the results were interesting. Figure 5.1 presents the Phoenix Park students' results alongside those from Amber Hill to demonstrate the difference in the shape of the two graphs. At Phoenix Park, the students' times produced a symmetrical distribution, indicating that when students were given the freedom to work (or not), some students did very little work but as many chose to do a lot. Indeed a much greater proportion of Phoenix Park students reported working for 51–60 minutes than Amber Hill students who were 'made' to work (12 per

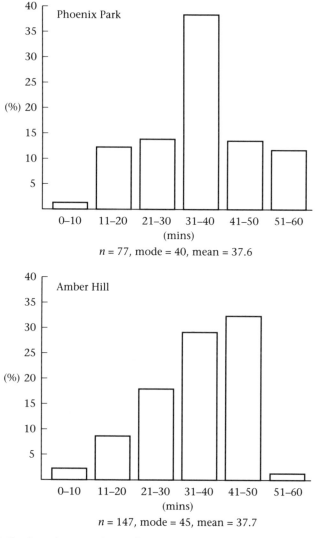

Figure 5.1 Students' perceptions of time spent working at Phoenix Park and Amber Hill

cent at Phoenix Park, 2 per cent at Amber Hill). Despite these differences, the means of the times given by Amber Hill and Phoenix Park students were identical (37 minutes). This, in some senses, is remarkable given the difference in the freedom experienced by the two sets of students.

Earlier I described the relaxed nature of Jim Cresswell's lessons and said that these lessons appeared to be more chaotic than those of Martin Collins and Rosie Thomas. However, the means of the times given by students of the three teachers at Phoenix Park were as follows: Rosie 40 minutes, Jim 39 minutes, Martin 32 minutes. Martin was reported by the students to be the strictest of the three teachers. The similarity between the times given by students of different teachers and the times of students at the different schools adds further weight to the idea that making students work is not a particularly effective way of getting students to think about mathematics.

The uninterested students

In every mathematics lesson I observed at Phoenix Park, between three and six students would do very little work and spend much of their time disrupting others. I shall now try and describe the motivation of these twenty or so students, who represented a small but interesting group. The students who did very little work in class were mainly boys and they related their lack of motivation to the openness of the mathematics approach and, more specifically, the fact that they were often left to work out what they had to do, on their own.

> S: I tend to doss about a lot in maths; half the time I can't be bothered to call miss over or ask her what I want to know, but I do realise that maths GCSE is pretty important.
>
> JB: Why do you mess about in maths more than other subjects?
>
> S: Because half the time if I ask for help I don't get it, or I don't get it until 20 minutes after I've asked.
>
> (Shaun, Phoenix Park, Year 10, RT)

Many of the students at Phoenix Park talked about the difficulty they experienced working on open projects that required them to think for themselves, when they first started at the school. But most of the students gradually adapted to this demand, whereas the disruptive students continued to resist it. In Years 10 and 11, I interviewed six of the most disruptive and badly behaved students in the year group: five boys and one girl. They explained their misbehaviour in lessons in terms of the lack of structure or direction they were given and, related to this, the need for more teacher help. These students had been given the same starting points as everybody else but, for some reason, they seemed unable, or unwilling, to think of ways to work on the activities without the teacher telling them what to do. This was a necessary requirement with the Phoenix Park approach, for it was impossible for all of the students to be supported by the teacher when they needed to make decisions.

The students who did not work in lessons were no less able than other students; they did not come from the same middle school and they were socioeconomically diverse. In questionnaires the students did not respond differently from other students, even on questions designed to assess learning-style preferences. The only aspect that seemed to unite the students was their behaviour and the fact that most of them were boys. The reasons that some students acted in this way and others did not were obviously complex and due to a number of interrelated factors. Martin Collins believed that more of the boys experienced difficulty with the approach because they were less mature and they were less willing to take responsibility for their own learning than the girls. The idea that the boys were badly behaved because of immaturity was also partly validated by the improvement in the boys' behaviour as they got older:

I: We have wasted a lot of time in the lessons, some of it, we have wasted time.

G: Yeah, we didn't used to do any work in lessons at all.

JB: But you take it more seriously now?

G: Yes.

JB: Why?

G: I'm not sure, in maths, then, we used to . . .

I: Chuck stuff.

G: Yeah we always used to be chucking stuff and fighting, now we're a bit more serious.

(Ian and Gary, Phoenix Park, Year 11, JC)

The misbehaving students in each group were generally streetwise, confident students, who seemed to enjoy being the centre of attention. It was as if they had decided that school work was not for them, but they could gain satisfaction and self-esteem from being part of an anti-school sub-culture. Other research studies have shown the presence of students with anti-school values who gain pleasure from misbehaving (Willis 1977; Ball 1981), but the Phoenix Park students experienced more freedom than students generally do in schools. The result of this freedom seemed to be that they did very little work. The students were also required to do a lot in mathematics lessons. They were not asked to work through pages of a book, following a rule. Instead they had to think for themselves and plan their work. They needed to make decisions and co-ordinate strategies. For many of the students, who were probably more inclined to 'mess about' than work when they arrived at the school, this was too much. As one of the girls, who shared lessons with them, commented:

Well I don't think they were stupid or anything, they just didn't want to do the work, they didn't want to find things out for themselves; they would have preferred it from the book; they needed to know straightaway sort of thing.

(Helen, Phoenix Park, Year 11, MC)

Although the students at Phoenix Park who did very little work in lessons were distinct from other students at the school, their behaviour in lessons was only a more extreme version of a behaviour displayed by most students at some times during lessons. The students worked when they wanted to work, which, for most students, meant intermittently.

But the tables that don't, even the tables that do get on with their work tend to jabber on a bit, like, Miss Thomas goes over to the table and she'll say, 'Oh did you see *Neighbours* last night?' to the other table and then they'll start talking and everyone will be talking.

(Shaun, Phoenix Park, Year 10, RT)

To summarize, it is probably fair to say that the students at Phoenix Park spent less time working than the students at Amber Hill, but more time engaged in their work. This was not true for all of the students, but the widespread lack of interest that was evident at Amber Hill was rarely witnessed at Phoenix Park. This was replaced by a much more varied response to work, which, for most students, included both times of involvement and times of non-mathematical activity.

Students' views about the nature of mathematics

The students at Phoenix Park were very different from the students at Amber Hill in the way that they viewed mathematics. This was because most of the students believed mathematics to be an active, enquiry-based discipline. In the Year 10 questionnaire item, mentioned in Chapter 4, that asked students to prioritize either thought or memory, 65 per cent of students at Phoenix Park chose thought, compared with 36 per cent of Amber Hill students. The students did not see mathematics as a rule-bound subject involving set methods and procedures that they needed to learn, they saw it as a subject of explorations, negotiations and enquiry:

> You explore the different things and they help you in doing that.
> (Alex, Phoenix Park, Year 11, JC)

> *P*: You can do it at your own level, what suits you, and it's very sort of open. You can use it in different ways, you can do different things more than with set questions.
> *S*: You're able to explore, there's not many limits and that's more interesting.
> (Philip and Simon, Phoenix Park, Year 11, JC)

The students also had a sense of mathematics as a subject that allowed them to think deeply, to go beyond surface features of questions:

> It's when you like learn new ways of doing things or you're like doing quite well on a problem . . . you're taking it really far, the investigation, you're getting really deep into it . . . you feel like you're learning quite a lot more.
> (Philip, Phoenix Park, Year 11, JC)

There is evidence that many students regard mathematics to be a collection of procedures that allow them to answer questions in a short space of time (Schoenfeld 1988). The Phoenix Park students did not seem to have this shallow view of mathematics; they were aware of the depth of the subject, the different layers that may be encountered. The students also demonstrated an unusual awareness of the diversity and breadth of mathematics. They did not regard mathematics as a vast collection of sums, they seemed to have a richer and more balanced view of the subject:

> *A*: I used to think that maths was just sums and hard work.
> *JB*: Don't you now?
> *A*: No, not really, some of it is, but there's a lot more stuff involved in it as well.
> *JB*: What other stuff?

> *A*: Well, different sorts of – well, there's loads of different things, theories and stuff like that, formulas, algebra, shapes and stuff.
>
> (Alex, Phoenix Park, Year 11, JC)

> *JB* Has doing the projects changed the way you think in any way?
> *D*: Yes 'cause like bookwork – say it's just all sums or whatever, but that's only like one really small part of maths, isn't it?
> *JB*: Mmm.
> *A*: If you're doing all problems and that you can learn about all the different areas. All the really advanced maths is a lot more to do with theorems and theories and that sort of thing than just sums.
>
> (Danny and Alex, Phoenix Park, Year 11, JC)

Neither Danny nor Alex particularly liked mathematics compared to their other school subjects, but this did not appear to affect the way in which they constructed their views about the *nature* of mathematics. Both students showed that they regarded mathematics as a diverse subject in which 'sums' were 'only one really small part'. In their Year 9 questionnaire, students were asked to describe one or more situations when they had used mathematics outside school. Seventy-seven per cent of the Amber Hill students' comments related to money or shopping and no descriptions were given of situations requiring the use of data handling, shape or space. At Phoenix Park, 53 per cent of comments also related to money and shopping but 14 per cent of students described non-numerical activities such as sorting out a magazine collection, classifying option choices at a club, laying slabs in the front garden, organizing a bank account, reading a map and organizing a route for a paper round. These were not examples that the students had been told about in class or contexts they had encountered in lessons.

In many of my lesson observations, the students approached mathematics and talked about mathematics in ways that were qualitatively different from most students I have observed in mathematics classrooms over the last ten years. They showed that they were not only interested in the answers to the investigations and problems they worked on, they were aware of the importance of the methods and processes which they used along the way:

> Sometimes I can't really think how things can be used, but it's the process and the method, I suppose, and the way you look at it.
>
> (Philip, Phoenix Park, Year 11, JC)

The students' awareness of the methods and processes they used in their work can probably be related back to the encouragement their teachers gave them to think about methods and strategies. Students were often asked to think about what they had been doing in lessons and to plan the direction of the rest of their work for homework. These homeworks stand in direct contrast to the more typical 'finish up to Question 20' mathematics homework. They explicitly required students to think about strategies and methods. In this extract Rosie Thomas is talking to John who has just solved a problem:

Rosie looks at John's work and says, 'Brilliant work John,' then 'but you can't just write it down, there must be some sense to why you've done it, some logic, why did you do it that way? Explain it.'

(Year 10, Rosie Thomas)

Rosie's 'there must be some sense to why you've done it' typifies the sort of encouragement the students were given at Phoenix Park. The teachers strove to *expand* the way in which the students thought about mathematics. They tried to extend the students' value systems beyond the desire to attain correct answers. There were many indications that the teachers were successful in this regard and that the unusually dynamic views the students held about mathematics were formed in response to their project-based work. All of the students contrasted this work with the SMP bookwork they encountered in middle school:

It's more interesting now, you're not just working through a book doing the same things.

(Helen, Phoenix Park, Year 10, RT)

You go right through the pages of a book until you've finished it and then it takes you to other pages, all pretty much the same stuff, you can't really experiment with work in books.

(Shaun, Phoenix Park, Year 10, RT)

It gives you more freedom here and it lets you find things out for your-self, where a book would just give you all the answers and stuff and you wouldn't have to find things out for yourself, you have to find things out for yourself and its more interesting and I think you tend to remember it more when you've found things out for yourself.

(Louise, Phoenix Park, Year 11, JC)

The students at Phoenix Park had all experienced a bookwork approach to mathematics prior to their project-based work and the contrast they offered between the two approaches focused upon the more dynamic nature of the mathematics they encountered in their project work. They talked about the way that books did not give them anything to 'find out' or 'explore', they merely gave them 'set work' that they had to 'work through'. The students highlighted the *procedural* aspect of bookwork which, they said, made mathematics less interesting and useful for them.

The significance of the students' project work to the active views of mathematics that they had developed was also demonstrated by the results of their Year 10 questionnaire. At Phoenix Park the students worked in an entirely open way until Christmas of Year 11 when they started preparing for examinations. At this time the mathematics approach became considerably more closed and the students were introduced to rules and formal methods and structures. When my case study year group were in Year 10, I gave a questionnaire to students in Years 9, 10 and 11. This included the question that asked students to prioritize either thought or memory. Sixty-six per cent of students completing Year 9 and 65 per cent of students completing Year 10 thought it was more important to think hard about questions, than remember similar questions. This proportion fell to 48 per cent of students completing

Year 11. At another point in the questionnaire the students were asked to rank different areas of mathematics in terms of importance. Five per cent of Year 9 students and 8 per cent of Year 10 students thought that 'remembering rules and methods' was the most important part of mathematics; in Year 11, this increased to 17 per cent of students. Responses to the same questions given to three year groups at Amber Hill remained constant between the three year groups (17 per cent, 15 per cent, 15 per cent).

The Phoenix Park students' responses to their Year 11 examination preparation indicate that the change from project work to a more formal mathematics approach prompted a corresponding change in the students' views about mathematics. Cobb *et al.* (1992) also found this to be true of students who worked on projects and who then reverted to a textbook approach. This caused many more of the students to think that success in mathematics involved following a teachers' set methods. At Phoenix Park, the project-based approach had expanded the students' views of mathematics and caused them to regard mathematics as an active, exploratory discipline. The examination work caused many students to go back to some of their old views about the limited nature of mathematics, thus eradicating some of the school's positive achievements.

Independence and creativity

The students at Phoenix Park were encouraged in many different ways to be independent in mathematics, mainly through the degree of choice they were given and the responsibility they needed to take for their work. In their Year 10 questionnaire, students were asked to describe mathematics lessons and 11 per cent of students *chose* to comment upon the independence they experienced in their lessons. For example, 'What you do is mostly up to the pupils.' None of the Amber Hill students responded in this way. When teachers interacted with students, they treated them as though they were equals. If they asked students to do something and the students asked why, they would explain rather than say, 'Because I said so.' The teachers did not seem to try and gain respect or deliberately distance themselves from students and the gap between teachers and students was not distinct. This seemed to have a direct effect upon the students. When they interacted with adults, even strangers, they were confident and chatty; they never appeared to be nervous.

When visitors walked into the classrooms at Phoenix Park, which was a common occurrence, the students appeared to be unconcerned whether they were inspectors, visiting dignitaries or parents. They would always chat to adults, run around, misbehave or swear at each other in the same relaxed manner, whoever was with them. When the head teacher walked into lessons, the students would not change their behaviour in any way and those who were not doing work would continue not to do work. In many of my conversations with students and observations of them around the school I was often reminded of Neill's Summerhill students. Neill attributed the confidence and ease with which these students treated adults to the progressive approach of Summerhill school which, he claimed, took away their fear and oppression (Neill 1985).

The independence and responsibility encouraged in the students seemed to have a direct effect upon their approach to mathematics. In a general sense the students seemed less oppressed and constrained than many students of mathematics and they seemed to take a more creative approach to mathematics than was normal for school students. In a questionnaire given to the students in Year 11, 82 per cent of Phoenix Park students agreed with the statement 'It is important in maths to use your imagination', compared with 65 per cent of Amber Hill students, a statistically significant difference. The students' creative approach to mathematics was demonstrated by the applied 'Planning a flat' activity I gave the students in Year 10. In this activity, the students were asked to design a flat in a given space and locate and draw the furniture in their flat. A major, but unexpected, difference between the students at Amber Hill and Phoenix Park related to the designs students produced. The students were invited to design a flat to suit a person or people of their choice, for example, a student, a couple, a family or themselves. The choice of rooms they would have in the flat was left entirely up to the students. All the students in both schools included in their designs at least one bedroom, bathroom, living room and kitchen. However, approximately one-third of the Phoenix Park students also included more unusual rooms. In the 89 designs produced by the students at Phoenix Park there were 35 examples of 'unusual' rooms with: seven games rooms, four football rooms (generally including small five-a-side pitches), three indoor swimming pools, three studies, two hi-fi rooms, two children's playrooms, two cocktail bars and one each of a bouncy castle room, a pool room, a Jacuzzi, a computer room, a gym, a garage, a bowling alley, a utility room, a piano room and a disco room. At Amber Hill, there were 99 flat designs which included two pool rooms, two swimming pools, one playroom and one store room. At Phoenix Park, the students included the rooms that they wanted to have in their flats; at Amber Hill, the students included the rooms that they thought that they *should* have, the rooms of which they felt a teacher or I would approve.

The lack of constraint the Phoenix Park students experienced in these different domains, and the lack of domination or control that was imposed by teachers, seemed to have contributed towards the confidence of the students at Phoenix Park, the creativity they demonstrated and the relaxed way in which they appeared to make and take decisions:

> That's the way I am . . . I just kind of do things in my own way, if it pulls off, it pulls off, if it doesn't then that's down to me.
>
> (Andy, Phoenix Park, Year 11, RT)

Summary

The mathematics approach of Phoenix Park was unusual, particularly because of its openness, the degree of choice the students were given, the independence students were encouraged to develop and the freedom the students had over their work environment and their work rate. These features of the mathematics approach should be located within the overall context of Phoenix

Park school, which was an unusually progressive institution that aimed to develop students' independence and decision-making abilities. The Phoenix Park approach to mathematics was different from the majority of schools because learning mathematics was not based around the learning of different mathematical procedures. Rather, the students were engaged in activities and projects in which the need for certain mathematical techniques became apparent. This approach necessitated a relaxation of the control teachers had over the structure and order of the classroom. The Phoenix Park teachers were not concerned about this, in line with their general approach to mathematics teaching and learning. Their concern was to give students mathematically rich experiences and to help them use mathematics, rather than to maintain order and a high work rate. They were concerned with the quality rather than the quantity of the students' mathematical experiences and with understanding rather than coverage. This meant that the Phoenix Park classrooms looked very different from those of Amber Hill and the experiences of the students were also markedly different.

At Phoenix Park, the students did not believe lessons to be uniform and monotonous. Instead, they regarded their lessons as varied and their enjoyment of lessons depended upon the particular activities they encountered. The students also displayed varied levels of engagement which differed between students as well as between lessons and parts of lessons. A small but important proportion of the year group at Phoenix Park misbehaved in lessons and said that they did not like the school's approach. However, it was difficult to know whether the students' lack of motivation caused their negative views about mathematics, whether it was the other way around or whether neither one caused the other.

Many of the Phoenix Park students regarded mathematics to be a dynamic, flexible subject that involved exploration and thought. They valued the importance of mathematical processes and the views they developed were, according to a wide range of literature (Erlwanger 1975; Doyle 1983; Schoenfeld 1988) extremely unusual. Additionally, the students displayed a freedom, creativity and lack of constraint in their interactions and behaviours which appeared to derive directly from the approach of the school.

In the next chapter, I shall present the results of various different assessments and consider the ways in which the difference between the two schools' approaches affected the students' understanding of mathematics.

6

Mathematical assessments

Introduction

There were many differences between the learning experiences of students at Amber Hill and Phoenix Park schools. At Amber Hill, the students were disciplined and hard-working and the mathematics they encountered was presented to them via a traditional, class-taught, transmission model of teaching. At Phoenix Park, the students spent less 'time on task' and they only learned about new mathematical methods and procedures when they needed to use these in their projects. In assessments of their mathematical knowledge and understanding, broad differences would therefore be expected between the two sets of students. In order to investigate whether differences existed in the extent, nature or form of students' understanding, I chose to use a variety of assessments. These included applied assessments, long-term learning tests, short contextualized questions and the GCSE examination. The different assessments involved are summarized in Table 6.1

Applied assessments

One of the aims of my study was to investigate Lave's notion of 'situated learning' (1988), in particular the ways in which students interacted with mathematics when it was encountered in different forms and settings. I knew that it would not be feasible to follow the students into mathematical situations in their everyday lives to do this, so I decided to give the students various applied activities within school. I then compared the students' responses to these activities with their responses to short, traditional tests that targeted the same areas of mathematics. Of course, the ways in which students react to applied tasks in school can never be used to predict the ways in which they will react to real-life mathematical situations. However, I believe that the degree of realism provided by applied tasks, combined with the artificiality of the school setting, provides important insight into the different factors that influence a student's use of mathematical knowledge.

Table 6.1 Overview of mathematical assessments

Timing	Form of assessment	Students involved	Research aim
Start of Year 9	Seven contextualized short questions	All case study cohort in both schools ($n = 305$)	To provide information on mathematical knowledge, use of mathematics in different contexts and a baseline measure of students' performances at the start of the research period.
End of Year 9	'Architectural' activity and related tests	Half of four groups in each school ($n = 104$)	To provide information on students' use of mathematics in an applied activity and their use of the 'same' mathematics in a short test.
Middle of Year 10	Long-term learning tests	Two groups in each school ($n = 61$)	To assess the students' knowledge of mathematics before it was taught, immediately afterwards and six months later.
End of Year 10	Nine contextualized short questions	All year group in both schools ($n = 268$)	To provide information on mathematical knowledge, use of mathematics in different contexts and changes in performance between Years 9 and 10.
	'Flat Design' and related tests	Four groups in each school ($n = 188$)	To provide information on students' use of mathematics in an applied activity and their use of the 'same' mathematics in a short test.
End of Year 11	Analysis of GCSE answers	All GCSE entrants in each school ($n = 290$)	Knowledge of mathematics, analysis of use of mathematics in conceptual/procedural questions.

The 'Architectural' activity

In the summer of their Year 9, approximately half of the students in the top four sets at Amber Hill ($n = 53$) and four of the mixed-ability groups at Phoenix

Park (n = 51) were asked to consider a model and a plan of a proposed house and to solve two problems related to local authority design rules. Students were given a scale plan, which showed different cross-sections of a house and a scale model of the same house. To solve the problems, students needed to find information from different sources, choose their own methods, plan routes though the task, combine different areas of mathematical content and communicate information. Because the students at Amber Hill were taken from the top half of the school's ability range and the students at Phoenix Park were not, there was a disparity in the attainment levels of the samples of students. The students in the Amber Hill sample had scored significantly higher grades on their mathematics NFER entry tests. However, my main aim was not to compare the overall performance of the students in the two schools, but rather to compare each individual's performance on the applied activity with their performance on a short written test. Approximately two weeks prior to the architectural task, the students took a pencil-and-paper test that assessed the areas of mathematical content that I anticipated they would need to use in the activity.

The 'Architectural' activity (Figure 6.1) comprised two main sections. In the first section, the students needed to decide whether the proposed house satisfied a council rule about proportion which stated that the volume of the roof of a house must not exceed 70 per cent of the volume of the main body of the house. The students therefore needed to find the volumes of the roof and of the house and find the proportion of the roof volume to the house volume. To do this students, could use either the scale plan or the model. The second council rule stated that rooves must not have an angle of less than 70°. The students therefore had to estimate the angle at the top of the roof, which was actually 45°, from either the plan or the model. This was a shorter and potentially easier task.

In designing the activity, I formed questions which would require students to combine and use different areas of mathematics together. The individual areas of mathematics that were involved (multiplication, division, area,

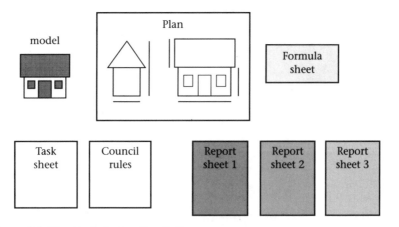

Figure 6.1 The 'Architectural' activity

volume, percentages, angles, measurement) were not particularly difficult and they had been encountered by all of the students in all classes, but the demand of the task related to the need to choose, combine and use different mathematical methods. Students had access to calculators at all stages of the activity.

Grades for the two sections were awarded as follows: a grade of 1 was given if the answer was correct or nearly correct, with one or two small errors; a grade of 2 was awarded if most or all of the answer was incorrect. All of the students made some attempt at the problems. In the test, the students were given three questions which assessed the mathematics involved in the proportion problem; they were asked to find the volume of a cuboid, the volume of a triangular prism (similar to the roof) and to calculate a percentage. Table 6.2 shows grades for the two aspects of the applied problem for students who answered the relevant test questions correctly. Table 6.3 shows grades for the two aspects of the applied problem for students who answered the relevant test questions incorrectly. Tables 6.2 and 6.3 show that in the roof volume problem, 29 Amber Hill students (55 per cent) attained the highest grade of 1, compared with 38 (75 per cent) of Phoenix Park students, despite the fact that the Amber Hill students were taken from the top half of the school's ability range. Table 6.2 also shows that at Amber Hill, 15 students (28 per cent) could do the mathematics when it was assessed in the test, but could not use it in the activity. This compared with 8 students at Phoenix Park (16 per cent). In addition Table 6.3 shows that 15 students (29 per cent) at Phoenix Park attained a grade 1 on the activity, despite getting one or more of the relevant test questions wrong, compared with 6 students (11 per cent) at Amber Hill.

Table 6.2 Problem results for students who answered the relevant text questions correctly

| | Volume | | | Angle | |
	Amber Hill	Phoenix Park		Amber Hill	Phoenix Park
Test grade 1	23	23	Test grade 1	31	40
Test grade 2	15	8	Test grade 2	19	8
Total	38	31	Total	50	48

Table 6.3 Problem results for students who answered the relevant text questions incorrectly

| | Volume | | | Angle | |
	Amber Hill	Phoenix Park		Amber Hill	Phoenix Park
Test grade 1	6	15	Test grade 1	3	2
Test grade 2	9	5	Test grade 2	0	1
Total	15	20	Total	3	3

In the test on angle, the students were given a 45° angle (the same angle as the roof in the activity) and asked whether it was 20°, 45°, 90° or 120°. Fifty Amber Hill students estimated this angle correctly in the test, but only 31 of these students estimated the 45° angle correctly in the applied activity. At Phoenix Park, 40 out of 48 students who recognized the angle in the test solved the angle problem. Paradoxically, the least successful students at Amber Hill were in set 1, the *highest* group. Ten of the 14 students in the top set did not solve the roof volume problem and nine of the 14 students did not solve the angle problem. In both of these problems, this failure emanated from an inappropriate choice of method. For example, in the angle problem, the ten unsuccessful students attempted to use trigonometry to decide whether the angle of the roof, which was 45°, was more or less than 70°, but they failed to use the methods correctly. Successful students estimated the angle using their knowledge of the size of 90° angles. Unfortunately, the sight of the word 'angle' seemed to prompt many of the Amber Hill set 1 students to think that trigonometry was required, even though this was clearly inappropriate in the context of the activity. The students seemed to take the word 'angle' as a cue to the method to use. Some of the students gained nonsensical answers from their misuse of trigonometry, such as 200°, but they did not realise that the 45° angle of the roof could not possibly have been 200°.

The students undertook the architectural activity and associated tests at the end of Year 9, one year after the start of their different approaches. At this stage, the difference between the mathematical behaviours of the two sets of students appeared to be emerging. This was particularly evident amongst students in sets 1 and 2 at Amber Hill who were less successful in the activity than students in sets 3 and 4. At Phoenix Park, the students were slightly less successful on the test questions, which could possibly be accounted for by the fact the students were taken from a significantly lower ability range, but the students were markedly more successful in the activities. The main problem that seemed to be experienced by the Amber Hill students related to an inability to decide what to do when they were not given explicit instructions. The students had learned appropriate mathematical methods, but when they were left to choose the methods to use, they became confused. The students in set 1 for example appeared to use trigonometry, rather than estimation, because the activity was about angles and they related angles to trigonometry. They were not able to see the inappropriateness of trigonometry within the situation.

'Planning a flat' activity

One year later, at the end of Year 10, all the students in the top four sets at Amber Hill (*n* = 99) and all the students in four mixed-ability classes at Phoenix Park (*n* = 89) were given a second applied activity and set of related tests. 'Planning a flat' was adapted from a GAIM activity of the same name (Graded Assessment in Mathematics 1988). Students worked on the activity and accompanying questions over the period of two consecutive lessons, each lesson lasting one hour. The activity and questions were given to complete classes. The students at Amber Hill were, again, of a significantly higher ability than the students at Phoenix Park, measured on NFER tests.

In the first lesson, students were given an A3 plan of an empty basement flat. The plan showed only the structural features of the flat – the external walls, windows, chimney breasts and the front door. The students were asked to decide upon the intended owners of the flat and then decide upon appropriate rooms to put into the flat. Students then needed to draw rooms, doors and furniture onto the A3 plan, using their knowledge of measurement and scale. On the A3 plan of the flat, students were given two important pieces of information. First, the scale of the flat was provided twice, in two different forms. A two centimetre line showed the size of one metre at the bottom of the flat plan and a box of information also gave the scale as 1:50 at the side of the plan. The second important piece of information concerned building regulations. A box at the bottom of the plan gave two regulations:

- Each 'habitable' room (i.e. living room, bedroom) must have a window in it.
- There must be two doors between a toilet and a kitchen.

Students were allowed to work together on the design of their flats if they wanted to, but they had to produce one design each.

In the second lesson, students were given two questions to answer, which related to their flats. The first question appeared in the students' instructions as follows:

Carpet costs about £7.99 per square metre.
(a) Roughly how much would it cost to carpet all of the flat? Show all your working out.
(b) The second question is reproduced in Figure 6.2.

Approximately one month before taking the activity and related questions, the students were given a short written test that assessed all of the mathematics which featured in the activity and related questions. In the short written test, the students from Amber Hill attained significantly higher grades

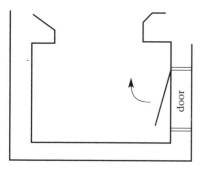

Figure 6.2 'Planning a flat' question
'Street doors must open to an angle of at least 115°. Will the street door of the flat pass this regulation? (The door is shown on the diagram.) You *must not* use an angle indicator – explain how you have worked out your answer.'

on questions assessing area, angle and percentage than the students at Phoenix Park; there were no significant differences on the question-assessing scale. These differences were mainly because of the high success rate of the set 1 students at Amber Hill on the tests; when these students were taken out of the sample, the only significant difference between the two schools occurred in the question on area. Despite the Amber Hill students' apparent competence with the mathematical procedures involved, the Phoenix Park students attained significantly higher grades on all sections of the applied activity and related questions.

The students' flat designs were assessed using the GAIM (1988) criteria for the activity. Grade 1 is the highest grade, grade 5 the lowest. High grades are given if students make correct measurements, use scale appropriately, take account of the building regulations and produce well-proportioned designs. The two groups of students produced the results in Table 6.4. These results show that there were vast differences between the performance of the students at the two schools, with students at Phoenix Park gaining significantly higher grades, despite the fact that the students were taken from a significantly lower-ability range. The main difference between the two schools was that 61 per cent of Phoenix Park students produced well-planned designs, with appropriately sized and scaled rooms and furniture, compared with only 31 per cent of Amber Hill students. Twenty-four per cent of the Amber Hill students drew rooms which were of an inappropriate size, or that contained wrongly scaled furniture and doors, compared with 6 per cent of the Phoenix Park students. This was despite the fact that 90 per cent of Amber Hill students successfully used scale in the short, written test.

Another major difference between the two schools was described in Chapter 5. This related to the types of rooms the students designed. As noted earlier, 33 per cent of the Phoenix Park students included unusual rooms such as disco rooms and bowling alleys in their flats, compared to approximately 3 per cent of Amber Hill students. In general, the inclusion of these more unusual rooms at Phoenix Park did not mean that the students produced unrealistic designs with inappropriately sized rooms. Many of the designs were very ingenious, entailing a creative use of space with interlocking rooms that saved on redundant hall or corridor space. In effect, the students often gave themselves a more demanding cognitive task, but managed to attend to the rules that they were given and the constraints of size and scale to produce impressive designs. This reflected a general and quite marked difference between the two schools. Many of the Amber Hill designs were inaccurate, sketchy and basic, despite the obvious commitment and enthusiasm shown by the students during the activity. The Phoenix Park designs were of a much higher standard, and they

Table 6.4 'Planning a flat' results (per cent). For Amber Hill, $n = 99$; for Phoenix Park, $n = 89$

School	1	2	3	4	5
Amber Hill	31	24	7	18	19
Phoenix Park	61	6	8	13	12

Table 6.5 'Area' question results (per cent). For Amber Hill, $n = 88$; for Phoenix Park, $n = 72$

School	1	2	3	4	5	6	7
Amber Hill	38	34	10	2	9	7	0
Phoenix Park	71	17	1	1	0	6	4

included designs and furnishings that were carefully and accurately constructed. Students at both schools reported enjoying the activity immensely, particularly the Amber Hill students, many of whom asked if they could do more work of a similar nature.

In the second lesson, the students were asked to answer the three questions which related to their flat designs. The first question asked the students how much it would cost, 'roughly', to carpet all of their flats, using carpet of a given price. Students attained grade 1 if they gave an appropriate estimation, grade 2 if they worked out the exact answer and grades 3–7, depending upon the number of mistakes they made.

In the question on area there were significant differences between the two schools, with 71 per cent of Phoenix Park students attaining the highest grade compared with 38 per cent of Amber Hill students (Table 6.5). Grade 1 was given for answers that gave a correct *approximation* of the cost of carpet, which was the requirement of the question. Grade 2 was given if the students calculated the exact area of the floor space of the flat, subtracting the space taken up by chimney breasts and other protrusions. Thirty-four per cent of Amber Hill students attained this grade. The decision to work with this degree of accuracy was not sensible in the context of the activity because carpet would need to be bought for the area including the chimney breast spaces. If these spaces were subtracted from the length of carpet bought, there would not be sufficient carpet for the flat. Quite apart from this constraint, the question asked the students to work out roughly how much the carpet would cost and the word 'roughly' was highlighted.

This response of the Amber Hill students was interesting because it demonstrated, again, the influence of certain goals or constraints upon the way in which students responded to the question. The students who used an exact measurement of floor space to answer the question did not show a good understanding of the demands of the context, even though they had worked on their designs for the entire previous lesson. This was probably because they were doing what they thought was expected of them, which meant working with the numbers and ignoring the situation or context in which they were placed.

In the final question, which asked whether the street door could open to an angle of at least 115°, grade 1 was given for correct answers and grades 2–4 for various incorrect answers. This question gave the results in Table 6.6. These results show that the Amber Hill students were relatively unsuccessful at estimating an angle within the context of a problem, despite the fact that 96 per cent of Amber Hill students successfully estimated a similar angle in the short, written test.

Table 6.6 'Angle' question results (per cent). For Amber Hill, $n = 89$; for Phoenix Park, $n = 71$

School	1	2	3	4
Amber Hill	43	16	39	2
Phoenix Park	75	10	10	6

The results of this applied activity reveal that there were significant differences between the performance of the students in the two schools in their flat designs, their use of area and their estimation of an angle. The lack of success amongst the Amber Hill students on various aspects of the activity was not caused by their lack of mathematical knowledge but appeared to derive from the goals the students formed in relation to the activity. In producing their flat designs, the Amber Hill students did not seem to work with the freedom of the Phoenix Park students. The Phoenix Park students produced more unusual and creative designs which were also more accurate and appropriately sized and scaled. The Amber Hill students may have failed to make use of their knowledge of scale and measurement because they had not been told to demonstrate that piece of knowledge in the activity. In the question on area, the Amber Hill students were able to work out the mathematical skills they should demonstrate and many of the students gave answers that were 'too' accurate for the situation or context. I interviewed ten of these students after the activity and asked them why they had done this. They said that they gave this degree of accuracy because they thought they had to 'show their maths'. The students demonstrated quite clearly the influence of non-mathematical goals upon their choice of mathematical procedure. If the students had been asked why they attempted to use trigonometry, rather than estimate the angle in the 'Architectural' problem they probably would have said the same thing – to show the skills that they had learned. A further 28 per cent of Amber Hill students were unable to work out an area of any accuracy, compared with 12 per cent of Phoenix Park students. In the question on angle, many of the Amber Hill students again failed to show their mathematical knowledge of angle that they had shown in the test.

The performance of the Amber Hill students on various aspects of the flat design task showed that they had difficulty making use of the mathematics they had learned in an applied situation. This did not appear to be due to a lack of mathematical knowledge, but the ways in which the students *interpreted* the demands of the activity. This will be considered in more depth in the next chapter. At Phoenix Park, the students performed well on all aspects of the task and related questions, despite the fact that the ability range of the students was lower than that of the students at Amber Hill.

Long-term learning tests

In this assessment, students were tested on a piece of their school work immediately before being taught the work (pre-test), immediately after completing the work (post-test) and then six months later (delayed post-test). On each of the three assessment occasions, the students took exactly the same test. The tests were designed to assess the learning that took place on a particular topic, in a similar style and format to the actual work. Because the Amber Hill students were taught in sets, their work was usually targeted at very specific levels of content. This made the design of the assessment questions straightforward. I essentially designed questions that were replicas of the questions they had worked on in their SMP textbooks, with different numbers and contexts. In Phoenix Park, the design of the assessment questions was extremely difficult because the students were of different 'abilities', working at different levels of mathematics. The results for the Amber Hill students are therefore more valid than those for the Phoenix Park students. For this reason, I will not expand upon this exercise in detail, but I have provided a summary of the results as, even with these limitations, they were interesting.

At Amber Hill, the two groups that were assessed were a Year 9 top set and a Year 10 set 4, both taught by Edward Losely. Both groups were taught using the typical Amber Hill approach with the teacher explaining methods on the board, followed by the students practising the methods in exercises. The top set group was taught at a relatively fast pace, as was normal for the school. Both groups worked for about three weeks on the topics that were assessed.

The experiences of the two groups at Phoenix Park differed in more fundamental ways. One group was a Year 9 that were working on what Martin Collins described as 'the most didactic piece of teaching' they ever did at the school. This consisted of Rosie Thomas teaching the students how to do long division without a calculator on the board and then letting them explore division patterns. The work lasted for only two lessons. The Year 10 work, also taught by Rosie, was a more typical Phoenix Park project on statistics, that lasted for about three weeks. A summary of the main results is given below:

- The least successful group of the four was the Year 9 top set group at Amber Hill. This group learned and remembered 9 per cent of the work they had been introduced to over a six-month period. The year 10 group learned and remembered slightly more of their work – approximately 19 per cent. This was despite the fact that the Amber Hill students were given tests that were exact replicas of their exercise book questions, with different numbers or contexts. At Phoenix Park the Year 9 group learned and remembered only 16 per cent of the work over a six-month period; the only group that was relatively successful was the Year 10 Phoenix Park group who remembered 36 per cent of the statistics they used during their open-ended projects.
- As the Phoenix Park tests had to be pitched in the middle of the group and some students may not have worked on aspects of mathematics that were assessed, a more fair comparison of the two schools is provided by the proportion of questions answered correctly in the post-test that were also answered correctly in the delayed post-test. These proportions are displayed in Table 6.7. The results of the long-term learning tests show that the Phoenix Park Year 10 students were more successful than students at Amber Hill and students who worked in a 'didactic' way at Phoenix Park. The results of the Amber Hill tests are particularly interesting as the close match between the

Table 6.7 Proportion of questions answered correctly in post-test also answered correctly in delayed post-test

School	Year 9	Year 10
Amber Hill	33%	50%
Phoenix Park	67%	83%

tests given to students and the work in their textbooks meant that the tests could give a relatively realistic picture of the students' learning. These tests showed that the Amber Hill students could remember a reasonable proportion of their work immediately after their lessons, but six months later, the Year 9 top set group had forgotten two-thirds of what they had learned and the Year 10 set 4 group had forgotten half of what they had learned.

Traditional mathematics assessments

Introduction

The superiority of the students' performance at Phoenix Park in applied mathematical assessments is probably not surprising, given the students' greater experience of open-ended mathematical activities in lessons. At Amber Hill, the students spent the vast majority of their time working through short, closed exercises assessing knowledge, rules and procedures that they had been taught by their teachers. Part of the reason that the school chose to teach in that way was to provide the students with a good preparation for examinations that assess mathematics in a similar format. This section will present the results of two different assessments which gave the Amber Hill students the opportunity to use the mathematics they had learned in a more familiar format.

Year 10 context questions

At the end of Year 10, the students were given the same short questions set in different contexts that were given to them at the beginning of the research study. These questions assessed conservation of number, number groups, fractions, perimeter and area. On the five questions which assessed fractions and conservation of number there were no significant differences between the schools. On the two number group questions the Amber Hill students attained higher grades, mainly because a large proportion of Phoenix Park students did not answer these questions. On the two questions involving perimeter and area the Phoenix Park students attained higher grades. Taken overall, the performance of the two sets of students on these tests was therefore broadly comparable – this result which was, in some senses surprising, will be illuminated further by a consideration of the students' performance on GCSE examinations.

Year 11 GCSE examinations

When the time came to take GCSE examinations, the Phoenix Park students faced many disadvantages. For example, during the majority of Years 9, 10 and 11, the students at Phoenix Park only learned about new mathematical procedures if they happened to need them during the course of a project. The students were also disadvantaged in the examination because Phoenix Park did not provide students with examination equipment such as calculators:

L: Like, the day before they told us all the equipment we needed and we had to go out and buy it and if you didn't have any money then you didn't have the equipment.
H: Like, it was your responsibility to take a calculator in, and that.
L: Yeah, like they usually supply them in lessons, then they didn't in the exam.
                                        (Linda and Helen, Phoenix Park, Year 11, MC)

The fact that the school did not lend the students calculators for the examination was fairly indicative of the school's relaxed approach to examinations in general. Martin Collins said that they could not supply calculators because the mathematics department did not have the money to buy them: they had bought enough calculators at the start of the year, but they could not replace those that were lost or stolen.

The students may also have been disadvantaged by the relaxed atmosphere of the school which meant that few of the Phoenix Park students were 'geared up' for their GCSE examinations. Indeed, many of the Phoenix Park students reported that they had not bothered with revision:

H: I can't say anyone I know is bothered about their GCSEs; I don't think we're revising or bottling down or anything; I think it hasn't hit us yet.
L: Yeah, I haven't done anything yet.
H: No, me neither.
L: Now I don't think I've got any time left to revise what's going to be in the exam and then you just leave it 'cause you don't know enough.
                                        (Helen and Linda, Phoenix Park, Year 11, MC)

At Phoenix Park, many of the students reported that the school's lack of attention to their examination needs disadvantaged them. The Amber Hill students' preparation for the examination was very different. The GCSE examination had a very high profile at Amber Hill and success in the examination was of primary importance to teachers and students alike. Indeed, the teachers at Amber Hill did not make any pretence of preparing students for more open, applied or realistic assessments of their knowledge. They were clear that their job was to prepare students for the GCSE examination in the best way possible. The students were also convinced of the aim of mathematics lessons and they reported that the high degree of motivation and hard work they demonstrated in lessons derived from their desire for GCSE success:

> JB: So if you all dislike it so much, why do you work so hard in lessons?
> C: Because we want to do well, maths GCSE is really important, everyone knows that.
>
> (Chris, Amber Hill, Year 11, set 4)

The pressure the students received to do well at Amber Hill may have disadvantaged them in the examination in the same way that the lack of pressure to do well may have diminished the capabilities of the Phoenix Park students. However, there were a number of indications that the Phoenix Park students faced a range of real and important disadvantages when they took their GCSE examinations, which the Amber Hill students did not have to contend with. These factors made the results from the two schools somewhat surprising.

At the end of Year 11, Amber Hill entered 182 of the 217 students on roll for GCSE mathematics; this amounted to 84 per cent of the cohort. At Phoenix Park, 108 of the 115 students on roll were entered for the examination; this was 94 per cent of the cohort. The two schools used different examination boards but Tables 6.8 and 6.9 give the results of the students at each school, as well as the national results for the different examination boards. Table 6.10 shows the A–C and A–G results from both of the schools.

The GCSE results at the two schools show that similar proportions of students at the two schools attained A*–C GCSE grades but significantly more Phoenix Park students attained A*–G grades. This was despite the similarity in the cohorts at the end of Year 8, the increased motivation of the Amber Hill students, the 'examination-oriented' approach at Amber Hill and the lack

Table 6.8 Amber Hill GCSE results

Parameter	A*	A	B	C	D	E	F	G	U	X	Y	n
Entry (n)	0	1	4	20	25	40	37	26	19	10	0	182
Entry (%)	0	0.5	2.2	10.9	13.7	22.0	20.3	14.3	10.4	5.5	0	182
Cohort (%)	0	0.5	1.8	9.2	11.5	18.4	17.1	11.9	8.8	4.6	0	217
National average	3.2	8.3	16.9	27.2	13.3	14.2	10.5	4.4	2.0	not available		100

Table 6.9 Phoenix Park GCSE results

Parameter	A*	A	B	C	D	E	F	G	U	X	Y	n
Entry (n)	1	2	1	9	13	28	27	20	5	1	2	108
Entry (%)	1	1.9	1	8.3	12	25.9	25	18.5	4.6	0.93	1.9	108
Cohort (%)	0.9	1.7	0.9	7.8	11.3	24.3	23.5	17.4	4.3	0.87	1.7	115
National average	0.2	2.0	7.3	15.1	16.8	18.4	16.5	16.2	7.5	not available		100

Table 6.10 Comparison of GCSE results (per cent)

Grade	Entry		Cohort	
	Amber Hill	Phoenix Park	Amber Hill	Phoenix Park
A*–C	13.7	12.0	11.5	11.3
A*–G	84.1	93.5	70.5	87.8
Percentage entered	84	94		

of calculators at Phoenix Park. Indeed, six Phoenix Park students wrote onto their actual GCSE papers, 'I haven't got a calculator', and at frequent points in the examination they wrote out the method they had used in the questions, but did not evaluate the answers, thereby losing marks. Despite these different factors, significantly more of the Phoenix Park students passed the GCSE examination than Amber Hill students. The A–C results for both schools were lower than national averages, but this would be expected from the intakes of the two schools. What would not perhaps have been expected was the similarity in A–C grades at the two schools, the increased proportion of A*/A grades at Phoenix Park (3 per cent of the Phoenix Park cohort compared with 0.5 per cent of the Amber Hill cohort) and the proportion of A–G passes at Phoenix Park, which was higher than the national average for the examination. However, I was not unduly surprised by the two sets of results or the superior performance of the Phoenix Park students. This was not because the students at Phoenix Park knew more mathematics – they clearly did not – but because they had developed a different *form* of knowledge and understanding.

During visits to the two examination boards, I recorded the marks that each student attained for every question on the GCSE examination papers. I had previously divided all of the questions into the categories 'procedural' and 'conceptual'. Procedural questions were those questions that could be answered by a simplistic rehearsal of a rule, method or formula. They were questions that did not require a great deal of thought if the correct rule or method had been learned. An example of such a question would be: 'Calculate the mean of a set of numbers.' Provided, of course, that students had learned how to calculate a mean, they did not have to decide upon a method to use, nor did they have to adapt the method to fit the demands of the particular situation. An example of a conceptual question was: 'A shape is made up of four rectangles, it has an area of 220 cm². Write, in terms of x, the area of one of the rectangles' (a diagram was given). Such a question requires the use of some thought and rules or methods committed to memory in lessons would not be of great help in this type of question. My rule in allocating questions was therefore: if the question could be answered from memory alone, it was procedural; if it also, or instead, required thought, it was conceptual. All the examination papers, from both examination boards, included both procedural and conceptual questions, with approximately twice as many procedural as conceptual. An analysis of the procedural and conceptual questions that students answered correctly and incorrectly in each school reveals a significant difference between the schools. The box and whisker plots given in Figures 6.3 and 6.4 show the distribution of the percentages of students attaining correct answers for the two different types of question at each school.

The conceptual questions were often, by their nature, more difficult than the procedural questions, even for a student who had both learned and understood mathematical rules and procedures. The students at both schools would

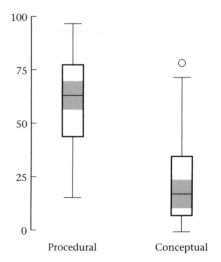

Figure 6.3 Percentages of students attaining correct answers for 'procedural' and 'conceptual' questions at Amber Hill

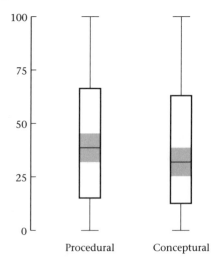

Figure 6.4 Percentages of students attaining correct answers for 'procedural' and 'conceptual' questions at Phoenix Park

therefore be expected to answer more of the procedural questions correctly. At Amber Hill, there was a significant difference between the percentages of students answering procedural and conceptual questions correctly, but at Phoenix Park, the percentages of students correctly answering the conceptual questions was, on average, only slightly lower than the percentages solving the procedural questions.

Students at both schools were entered for one of three levels of GCSE paper – higher, intermediate or foundation. At Phoenix Park, the students who answered the greatest proportion of conceptual, as opposed to procedural, questions correctly were those who took the higher level examination (same number of each type), followed by the intermediate-level students (nine conceptual questions for every ten procedural questions), followed by the foundation level students (six conceptual questions for every ten procedural questions). This trend across the three levels of paper may simply reflect the nature of mathematical confidence and ability, with the more competent students, entered for the higher papers, being more willing and able to tackle questions with a conceptual demand. However, at Amber Hill, it was the *intermediate*-level students who answered the highest proportion of conceptual questions (eight conceptual questions for every ten procedural), followed by the foundation and higher-level students (five conceptual questions for every ten procedural questions). Thus the higher-level Amber Hill students went against the trend displayed by the other students. At Amber Hill, all the higher-level students were taught in the top set and it seems likely that the speed at which they encountered work and the closed and rule-bound nature of their experience may have inhibited their performance on these questions. Chapters 9 and 10 will develop the idea that the top-set students at Amber Hill were disadvantaged by their placement within this set.

Analysis of the different questions answered correctly by students taking the different levels of paper also reveals that whilst similar proportions of students at both schools attained grades A–C, these grades were achieved in different ways. The higher-level students at Amber Hill correctly answered two procedural questions for every one conceptual question, whereas the higher-level Phoenix Park students attained equal numbers of each question correct. The main source of disadvantage for the potential A–C grade students at Amber Hill seemed, therefore, to be the conceptual questions, which took up approximately one-third of the examination paper. At Phoenix Park, the students attained equal proportions of each question correct, even though many of the conceptual questions were quite demanding. This suggests that the Phoenix Park students would have performed much better at this level if they had been taught more of the procedures that were assessed in the examination. The responses of the students who could have attained A–C grades also indicated that their lack of knowledge of formal procedures fazed them in the examination:

There were loads we hadn't done, weren't there? There were all those ones with weird equations that we'd never seen.

(Lindsey, Phoenix Park, Year 11, JC)

The main source of disadvantage for the potential A–C students at Phoenix Park seemed to be their lack of procedural knowledge, which was important because the procedural questions took up two-thirds of the examination paper. Despite this, the overall attainment of the two sets of students was broadly equivalent.

A consideration of the proportion of students attaining grades A–G at each school shows that the Phoenix Park students were significantly more success-ful. At Amber Hill, only 84 per cent of entrants and 71 per cent of the cohort attained grades A–G, compared with 94 per cent of Phoenix Park entrants and 88 per cent of their cohort. Indeed, the A–G results for Phoenix Park were better than national averages, even though the achievement of the cohort was considerably lower than the national average on entry to Phoenix Park. The distribution of grades in each school shows that this difference seemed to be largely due to the fact that more of the Phoenix Park students who were entered for the examination attained grades E, F and G (57 per cent at Amber Hill, 69 per cent at Phoenix Park), whereas more of the Amber Hill students failed the examination (16 per cent at Amber Hill, 7 per cent at Phoenix Park). This was despite the fact that Amber Hill did not enter 35 (16 per cent) of their students and Phoenix Park entered all but seven (6 per cent) of their students. These results give clear evidence of a superior performance from the students at Phoenix Park, particularly those students who were entered for the foun-dation-level papers. An examination of the types of questions answered across the foundation-level papers shows that students at both schools answered cor-rectly approximately two procedural questions for every conceptual question. Thus the Phoenix Park students did not attain higher grades because they answered more of a particular type of question correctly, they attained higher grades because they answered more of *both* of these types of question correctly. One source of disadvantage for the Amber Hill students was probably the fact that the students who should have got grades E, F or G were in low sets, whereas the Phoenix Park students were in mixed-ability groups. This will be considered in more detail in Chapter 10. The other likely source of disadvan-tage for the Amber Hill students was simply that they had developed a less effective mathematical understanding and this will be considered in more detail in Chapter 7.

At Phoenix Park there were a group of badly behaved and apparently un-motivated students in the year group. However, a comparison of NFER entry results and GCSE results showed that these students did not underachieve, in relation to other students, on the GCSE examination. This could mean that the students engaged with their mathematics for at least some of the time and that their bad behaviour (and other students' good behaviour) was a less effec-tive measure of their mathematical learning than would normally be assumed. A comparison of the three teachers at Phoenix Park also showed that the students in Jim Cresswell's groups, who experienced the most freedom, per-formed as well, or better, than the students in the classes of Martin Collins and Rosie Thomas, the 'stricter' teachers, even though all groups had a similar attainment range when they began Phoenix Park.

An overall consideration of the GCSE results indicates that if Amber Hill and Phoenix Park's approaches were to be evaluated in terms of examination success alone, the Phoenix Park approach must be considered to be more successful. This is despite the fact that the Phoenix Park students were not used to examinations and their school's approach could not, in any sense, be regarded as examination-oriented. A consideration of the students' performance on procedural and conceptual questions on the GCSE examination shows that the students at the two schools attained broadly similar grades, in different ways. The Amber Hill students were much more successful on the procedural questions, which suggests that their examination performance would be enhanced if they were able to think about, and solve, more of the conceptual questions. The development of this capability would probably also advantage students in many other situations, because the conceptual questions required a depth of thought that would be useful in a number of applied and 'real-world' settings. The Phoenix Park students would probably achieve greater examination success if they learned more of the standard mathematical procedures that are assessed in the GCSE examination, but it seems unlikely that this would advantage the students in any other situation than a mathematics examination. This raises questions about the appropriateness of the mathematics assessed in the GCSE examination, an issue to which I shall return in the final chapter.

Discussion and conclusion

I would like to suggest that the results of all of the assessments that have been reported in this chapter were broadly consistent. These showed that the Phoenix Park students had developed a mathematical understanding that they were more able to make use of than the Amber Hill students. This was demonstrated in various applied situations and conceptual GCSE questions. Even within more traditional assessments, the Phoenix Park students performed as well, or better, than the students at Amber Hill. I believe that these results were all indications of the same phenomenon: the students at the two schools had developed a different *kind* of mathematics knowledge. The Phoenix Park students did not have a greater knowledge of mathematical facts, rules and procedures, but they were more able to make use of the knowledge they did have in different situations. The students at Phoenix Park showed that they were flexible and adaptable in their use of mathematics, probably because they understood enough about the methods they were using to utilize them in different situations. The students at Amber Hill had developed a broad knowledge of mathematical facts, rules and procedures that they demonstrated in their textbook questions, but they found it difficult remembering these methods over any length of time. Also, they did not know enough about the different methods to base decisions on when or how to use them or adapt them. Further evidence of these important differences in the students' behaviour towards mathematics will be presented in the next chapter which will also relate the apparent differences in the students' knowledge and understanding to the approaches of the two schools.

7

Analysing the differences

Introduction

In Chapter 6, I presented the results of a number of different forms of assessment. These assessments, taken together, seem to indicate some important differences between the learning of the students at the two schools. I will now suggest that whilst the performance differences on these assessments were not always large, they in fact reflected an important variation in the nature of the students' understanding.

Amber Hill

Performance patterns

There was evidence from both lesson observations and the assessments shown in Chapter 6 that the students at Amber Hill were able to use the mathematical knowledge they had learned when the requirements of questions were explicit. This meant that they could work through their exercises in class with relative ease, they performed well on all of the short, written tests that accompanied the applied activities and they were able to answer many of the procedural GCSE questions. The difficulties seemed to occur for the students when the requirements of questions were not explicit, when they needed to use some mathematics after a period of time, when they had to apply mathematics and when they needed to combine different forms of mathematics. I believe that these difficulties occurred because of a combination of the nature of the students' understanding of mathematics and the perceptions that the students had developed about mathematics.

At Amber Hill, many of the mathematics lessons were rapidly paced, closed and procedural. This seemed to have had a clear impact upon the students, causing them to develop a shallow, procedural kind of knowledge, and a perception that mathematics was all about learning and remembering rules and formulae. Neither the students' views nor the procedural nature of their learning were surprising given that the students had time in lessons only to try and learn methods; they did not have the time, nor did they receive the encouragement, to think about them deeply. The students themselves became concerned about their mathematical performance when they took their mock GCSE examinations. Until that time, they had thought that they would be successful in mathematics if they learned all the rules and formulae they were introduced to in their lessons. In the mock GCSE examination the students found that this was not the case:

> It's stupid really 'cause when you're in the lesson, when you're doing work – even when it's hard – you get the odd one or two wrong, but most of them you get right and you think, 'Well when I go into the exam I'm gonna get most of them right,' 'cause you get all your chapters right. But you don't.
>
> (Alan, Amber Hill, Year 11, set 3)

The students encountered a variety of problems in both the mock and actual GCSE examinations. For example, they could not remember many of the procedures they had learned over time. This was demonstrated by the long-term learning assessments and supported by the students' comments in interviews:

> S: Usually, like I know that pi is equal to 3.14 because it's easy to remember but I don't actually remember like the diameter, how to find out the diameter of a circle 'cause we done that a few weeks ago.
> B: No I can't remember that, like the circumference and the radius.
> S: I wouldn't know now how to think about it, like we done that what about three weeks ago? And I could do it when we finished it but I don't think I'd remember it now.
>
> (Sam and Bridget, Amber Hill, Year 10, set 3)

Many of the Amber Hill students talked in similar terms about the difficulty they experienced using mathematics after a period of time. Sam's comment gives some indication of the reason for this, because she said that she 'wouldn't know now how to think about it', suggesting that because her memory of the procedure had gone, she would not be able to think about the mathematics. This suggests that students were disadvantaged in two related ways. First they experienced difficulties because of their belief that they had to rely upon their memory in order to solve mathematical problems. Then they experienced difficulties because the ways in which they had learned methods had not given them access to a depth of understanding that helped them to remember methods. This meant that students had problems even when they were presented with straightforward questions that assessed isolated mathematical concepts in forms that were very familiar to them. For example, 93 per cent of students who took the intermediate GCSE paper answered a question on simultaneous equations. All of these students attempted to use the standard procedure they had learned, but only 26 per cent of students used the procedure correctly. The rest of the students used a confused and jumbled version of the procedure and received no marks for the question.

A second problem was experienced by students when they needed to use different types of mathematics within the same activity. For example, in the first part of the roof problem in the 'Architecture' activity (pp. 65–8) students needed to use measurement, scale, volume and percentage. The combination of these methods in the same problem seemed to cause difficulties for the Amber Hill students and the students reported similar difficulties in the GCSE examination:

> M: 'Cause in the exam, we only had about two of them questions from class, in the whole exam – probably the whole Year got them right.
>
> JB: What sort of questions – when you say there were only two of them, what sort were they?
>
> M: Like, if you have this and that number and then, how do you do it?
>
> JB: So, what was the rest of the exam if it wasn't that?
>
> M: It was jumbled up, it was like ratio and then it was like digits and then the next question was that then it went back to ratios again, then it went to bearings, then it went to that and that, you see?
>
> (Marco, Amber Hill, Year 11, set 4)

When the Amber Hill students worked through their textbooks they learned one procedure and then practised it; in the examination, they needed to think about and combine different procedures and flexibly switch between different procedures in different questions. This caused difficulties for many of the students.

A third, and even bigger, problem was created for the students in situations when they needed to apply the methods they had learned. This was clearly demonstrated by the two applied assessments reported in Chapter 6. These showed that students successfully used knowledge in tests, but failed to make use of the 'same' knowledge in more applied activities. In the GCSE examination, the students also reported that they were unable to apply the methods they had learned:

> Some bits I did recognize, but I didn't understand how to do them, I didn't know how to apply the methods properly.
>
> (Lola, Amber Hill, Year 11, set 3)

Thus, even when students knew they had learned an appropriate piece of mathematical information, they could not do anything with it.

The difficulties the students experienced all seemed to relate to, or fit within, an overarching phenomenon which concerned the way in which students interpreted the demands of situations. This interpretation of experience seemed to be important, partly because it governed the way in which students responded to different situations and partly because it seemed to characterize the real difference between the learning of the students at the two schools.

Interpreting the demands of situations

In the 'Architecture' problem described in Chapter 6, a number of the Amber Hill students did not calculate the volume or the angle of the roof correctly. This was not because they could not perform calculations with volume or angle, but because they needed to interpret the question in order to determine what to do. Many of the students were unsuccessful because they saw the word 'angle' and thought that they should use trigonometry; it was their interpretation of the demands of the situation that failed them. There were other indications that the Amber Hill students were unsuccessful in the two applied situations that they were given in Year 9 and Year 10, because these required them to interpret the activities and decide what to do. This confusion was similar to the confusion students experienced when they moved between different exercises in their textbooks. They could perform the mathematical procedures, but they could not work out what was needed.

In the examination, this was also a major concern for students and students related many of their difficulties to the fact that the examination questions did not contain any cues in the way that their textbook questions did. In the textbook questions the students always knew what method to use – the one they had just been taught on the board – and if a question required something different or additional to this, there was always some clue in the question that would indicate what they had to do. In the examination, the questions did not simply require a precise and simplistic rehearsal of a rule, they required them to understand the questions and to know what the questions were asking them:

> We had one question, didn't we, and it's got like, what was it?, something stupid like . . . it was symmetry, you know, lines of symmetry, we had to change it round and it was, oh, it just said like, I've forgotten what it said now, but it had like this sentence and you thought – 'What do I do?' It didn't explain what you had to do in the paper and it was about 9 marks for that and you lost 9 marks just because it didn't tell you what to do.
>
> (Andy, Amber Hill, Year 11, set 3)

> Yeah in the exam it's like essays and that and . . . questionnaires . . . they're like misleading, and it's the same with graphs, they're misleading, graphs, and the questions, they're really misleading and if you can't understand one part you can't get the next part, and then you start panicking, but in the book and in the class it more or less explains itself.
>
> (Gary, Amber Hill, Year 11, set 3)

In their textbook lessons, the students had not experienced these demands, for the textbook questions always told them 'what to do'; they always followed on from a demonstration of a principle, method or rule. Unfortunately, the textbook questions never, at any point, required students to decide upon a method to use and, as Gary said, 'in the book and in the class it more or less explains itself'.

The students' inability to succeed on questions that did not indicate the 'correct' procedures to use can be related back to the students' belief that mathematics was a rule-bound, memory-based subject. The students could not think about and decide what was required of them in the examination because they believed that thinking was not what they were meant to be doing.

> Yeah you have to learn it so that you can tell the difference in the question as to which rules you use.
>
> (Sara, Amber Hill, Year 11, set 3)

They had been trained to learn rules and to spot clues in questions, rather than to interpret situations mathematically:

> In maths you have to remember, in other subjects, you can think about it, but in exams the questions don't really give you clues on how to do them.
>
> (Lorna, Amber Hill, Year 11, set 1)

In this extract, Lorna described quite clearly the problem she faced. She could not think about the requirements of the question, because 'in maths you have to remember', but how was she supposed to remember when the question did not contain any clues? Other students also described the difficulties they experienced when the clues or cues they were used to were absent:

> G: You can get a trigger, when she says like simultaneous equations and graphs, graphically, when they say like . . . and you know, it pushes that trigger, tells you what to do.
> JB: What happens in the exam when you haven't got that?
> G: You panic.
>
> (Gary, Amber Hill, Year 11, set 3)

In the mock examination, some of the teachers even gave students the cues they needed to answer the questions:

> My mind just went totally blank and I was really scared, a total blank, and I just couldn't focus, my concentration went completely and I just sat there like this . . . and I asked a question and said 'Can you read it to me and explain a bit more' and, without breaking the regulations she told me what it was about and I went, '*Oh, yeah*, I remember now' . . . and afterwards Miss Neville said to me, 'you *know* that and – well, sometimes you just need something to give you that little push, something to make you twig what it's about.'
>
> (Liam, Amber Hill, Year 11, set 3)

After the examination Liam's teacher said 'You *know* that' to him because Liam knew how to operate the procedure – but he did not know which procedure to use or why. All of the students interviewed in Year 11 ($n = 24$) were convinced that this was a real problem – they could not interpret the demands of the examination questions, they knew mathematical rules and procedures, but they could not make use of them. Some of the students described this as being unable to apply their mathematics, some talked about the absence of cues, others talked about not knowing the procedure to use. But they were all describing different aspects of the same problem; they could not use the methods they had learned unless the requirements of questions were explicit:

> 'Cause you haven't got a book . . . and so you've got to think of it and you think of it, but you think – 'But it could be', and then you think of about twenty different things it could be and you've got to decide which one.
>
> (Sara, Amber Hill, Year 11, set 3)

The students' responses to the examination seemed to be consistent with the mathematical behaviour they demonstrated in the assessments reported in Chapter 6.

Using mathematics in the 'real world'

I would like now to link the Amber Hill students' responses to the GCSE examination and their responses to the applied and long-term assessments to the way in which they used mathematics in non-school settings (see also Boaler 1996). When the students were in Years 10 and 11, I asked all of the students I interviewed ($n = 76$) to think of situations when they used mathematics outside school and to tell me whether they made use of school-learned methods in these situations. The Amber Hill students, like the adults observed in other research settings (Lave *et al.* 1984; Masingila 1993; Nunes *et al.* 1993), all said that they abandoned school mathematics and used their own methods:

> *JB:* And when you use maths in situations outside of school, do you use the methods you have learned in school or do you tend to use your own?
>
> *D:* You use your own.
>
> *S:* Yeah, you use your own.
>
> (Dean and Scott, Amber Hill, Year 10, set 4)

> *S:* I use my own methods.
>
> *JB:* Why?
>
> *S:* It's easier, 'cause I know how to do it myself then don't I? it makes more sense.
>
> (Sacha, Amber Hill, Year 11, set 4)

> *P:* No, you use your own methods.
>
> *D:* Yeah, your own methods.
>
> (Paula and Danielle, Amber Hill, Year 10, set 2)

Previous research on the way in which adults have used mathematics in different settings has demonstrated that adults were unable to use much of the mathematics they learned in school in 'real-world' situations (Lave 1988). These students suggest that they could not use the methods that they had learned in school in 'real-world' situations, even when they were still at school. This is probably not surprising given that students said that they could not remember the mathematics they had learned a few weeks after learning it, when they needed to use it in another chapter of their books, in the same social situation with similar mathematical demands. But the students did not only choose their own methods over their school-learned methods because they could not remember or use school-learned mathematics. They chose not to use school-learned methods because of the way they interpreted the demands of the 'real world'. The students at Amber Hill believed the mathematics they encountered in school and the mathematics they met in the 'real world' to be completely and inherently different. When I asked the students whether they believed the demands of the classroom and the 'real world' presented any similarities, they all reported that they did not:

> *JB:* When you use maths outside of school, does it feel like when you do maths in school or does it feel. . . ?

K: No, it's different.

S: No way, it's *totally* different.

(Keith and Simon, Amber Hill, Year 11, set 7)

The students analysed these differences in interesting ways:

J: They seem more important, worth doing, the things you do outside of school.

JB: Why is that?

J: Because you are doing it for yourself.

(John, Amber Hill, Year 10, set 1)

G: I use my own methods.

S: Yeah.

JB: Why is that do you think?

G: 'Cause when we're out of school yeah, we think, when we're out of school it's social, you're not like in school, it tends to be social, so it would be like too much change to refer back to here.

(George and Simon, Amber Hill, Year 10, set 3)

R: It's different 'cause you're like you're doing it your own way and you're relying on yourself to get it right.

D: Yes I think it's different 'cause, like he says, you do it in a different way.

(Richard and David, Amber Hill, Year 11, set 2)

S: It's different 'cause you have to work it out for yourself, like, you haven't got a book to show you what you've got to do.

(Shaun, Amber Hill, Year 11, set 1)

The clarity of the students' perceptions on this issue is quite striking, as, although there was no clear consensus about the reasons for the differences between mathematics in and out of school, all the students interviewed believed that using mathematics within school was a very different experience from using mathematics outside school. Furthermore, the students gave reasons for their ideas of difference which were very close to the ideas proposed by various researchers in the field. George, in set 3, was particularly interesting because he cited the influence of the social situation as the reason for his use of his own methods, in preference to school methods. Lave (1988) has noted the influence of the social situation over adults' choice of methods but George was not only influenced by the social situation, he was also aware of this influence. This suggests that his ideas of meaning and understanding in mathematical situations were very strongly influenced by the social nature of the settings and his statement that 'you're not like in school, it tends to be social, so it would be like *too much change* to refer back to here' gives a clear indication that his perceptions of the environments created by the 'real world' and the mathematics classroom were inherently different.

John in set 1 also concurs with researchers such as Cobb (1986) when he says that: 'They seem more important, worth doing, the things you do outside of school.' This student was able to cite the influence of his motivational goals upon his choice of method which, again, suggests that these goals had a strong influence upon him. It was clear from the students' description that their use of mathematics in situations within and outside school was goal-driven and that the goals formed were not inherently mathematical. They described the importance of situations outside school, the lack of complication, the social nature of the 'real world' and being alone, without books or teachers to help them. These differences caused the students to abandon their school-learned methods. However, although they showed that they did not make use of school methods in out-of-school situations, they were at least able to think for themselves and invent their own methods. Other students at Amber Hill painted a bleaker picture of their use of mathematics, indicating that their mathematical learning had disempowered them in more insidious ways, even stopping them from inventing their own methods:

JB: When you use maths outside of school, do you feel the same way as when you are doing maths in school or do they feel different?

J: They feel a lot different, like, um, you sort of have a little bit of understanding when you're in your lessons but your mind goes totally blank when you're outside.

JB: Why is that do you think?

J: You're not around people that understand it, like that can explain it to you and you're just like on your own . . . and you haven't got your little book with your notes.

(Jackie, Amber Hill, Year 10, set 1)

Schoenfeld lists seven 'typical' student beliefs, one of which is 'the mathematics learned in school has little or nothing to do with the real world' (Schoenfeld 1992: 359). The views of the Amber Hill students seemed to concur with this assertion. These views clearly limited the usefulness of their school-learned mathematics and I will continue my analysis of the different reasons for this in Chapter 8. Before doing so, I would like to consider the responses of the Phoenix Park students to the different assessments reported in the last chapter and to their GCSE examination.

Phoenix Park

Performance patterns

The results of Chapter 6 provide some indication that the students at Phoenix Park were at least as capable in test situations as the students at Amber Hill. In long-term assessments, many more of the Phoenix Park students who had learned mathematics via projects were able to answer questions correctly six months after their lessons. The difference in performance between the students at the two schools and the difference between Phoenix Park students in Year 9 and Year 10 on the long-term assessments indicates that this was due to the way in which students had learned their mathematics. When the students were introduced to standard methods and procedures that they practised, rather than used, they did not remember many of the procedures six months later. The students who had forgotten the largest proportion of their work (the Amber Hill Year 9, set 1 students) were introduced to their methods at a fast pace, which was probably a contributory factor. The only learning that seemed to have been moderately successful in the long term was that of the Phoenix Park Year 10 students, who learned about estimation and statistics when they used these ideas within an applied activity.

In the two applied assessments, the Phoenix Park students did not demonstrate the particular problems that the Amber Hill students demonstrated and the difference in performance of the students at the two schools became more marked as they experienced more of their different school approaches. In Year 9, many of the students at the two schools demonstrated a similar ability to solve problems related to angle and volume, apart from a significant proportion of the high set Amber Hill students who did not appear to interpret the demands of the situation well. In Year 10, the differences were more striking and the Phoenix Park students were significantly more able to produce good flat designs that incorporated their knowledge of measurement and scale, and then successfully solve problems related to angle and area. They also demonstrated a freedom in approach that the Amber Hill students did not seem to possess. I would now like to propose that the enhanced success of the Phoenix Park students derived from a capability and willingness that they had developed to think mathematically in different situations and to interpret the demands of varied settings.

Interpreting the demands of situations

At Phoenix Park, the students were interviewed in Year 11 a few weeks after completing their mock GCSE examinations. At this time, the students had experienced a few weeks of their examination preparation approach. This meant that projects had been abandoned and students had moved to a more formal and procedural system of learning. In interviews, the students reported that they found the GCSE mock examination difficult, but the students' concerns, which were reported in Chapter 6, were completely different from those expressed by the Amber Hill students. The students were concerned that the examination included mathematical notation and content areas that they had not met before, that their projects were difficult to revise from, that they did not receive any pressure to revise and, for some of them, that they did not have calculators. Despite the differences between the nature of the students' project work and the GCSE examination, the students at Phoenix Park did not report that they could not apply the methods they had learned, nor that they could not interpret the questions when they did not contain clues. Rather, the students reported that when they had learned the mathematics assessed, they were able to make use of it:

JB: How did you get on in your mocks?
H: OK, it wasn't really hard.
JB: Did you find that the questions were different to what you were used to?

H: Well a lot of the stuff we hadn't done, until now, that's what we're
    doing now.
JB: And when you came across a question where it was something you
    had done, did you feel you were able to do the question?
H: Yes, I found it easy.

(Hannah, Phoenix Park, Year 11, JC)

The Amber Hill students that were given similar interview questions
responded very differently:

JB: And what about the questions that you *could* remember doing, when
    you recognized what to do, did you feel able to do those questions?
C: I still couldn't do them, because they were different, I couldn't apply
    the methods properly.

(Carly, Amber Hill, Year 11, set 1)

The reports of the students at Phoenix Park given in Chapter 6 show that they
faced a number of disadvantages that may have diminished their examination
performance, but they still attained higher grades than the Amber Hill
students. The reason for this appeared to be that students could make use of
the mathematics they had learned when it was assessed and even though they
had not covered everything they needed for the examination, they could
make effective use of the mathematics they had encountered before. The
superior performance of the Phoenix Park students on conceptual questions
also provides an important clue as to the reason for their general success. The
students were able to use mathematics in different situations because of their
attitudes towards and beliefs about mathematics. When the students
approached questions, they believed that they should consider the situations
presented and interpret what they needed to do:

JB: Can you tell me about anything you like about maths?
T: I think it allows . . . when you first come to the school and you do
    your projects and it allows you to think more for yourself then when
    you were in middle school and you worked from the board or from
    books.
JB: And is that good for you do you think?
T: Yes.
JB: In what way?
T: It helped with the exams where we had to . . . had to think for our-
    selves there and work things out.

(Tina, Phoenix Park, Year 11, RT)

The students were not inhibited in the way that the Amber Hill students
were. They were not struggling to remember specific procedures, nor search
for cues which might indicate the procedures to use. They were free to consider the different questions and make sense of them:

JB: Did you feel in your exam that there were things you hadn't done
    before?
A: Well, sometimes I suppose they put it in a way which throws you, but
    if there's stuff I actually haven't done before I'll try and make as much

sense of it as I can, try and understand it and answer it as best as I can, and if it's wrong, it's wrong.

(Angus, Phoenix Park, Year 11, RT)

The Phoenix Park students were willing to try and think mathematically about questions and work out what was needed. This willingness appeared to derive from their belief in the value of thought in mathematics. Unlike the Amber Hill students, they did not believe that mathematical success depended upon learning different procedures:

JB: Is there a lot to remember in maths?
S: There's a lot to learn, but then you need to know how to understand it and once you can do that, you can learn a lot.
P: It's not sort of learning is it? It's learning how to do things.
S: Yes, you don't need to learn facts; in the beginning of the maths paper they give you all the equations and facts you need to know.

(Simon and Philip, Phoenix Park, Year 11, JC)

This extract is particularly important because Lave (1996a) has claimed that notions of knowing should be replaced with notions of doing, in order to acknowledge the *relational* nature of cognition in practice. These students seemed to support this relational view of knowledge, as illustrated by the distinction drawn out by Paul: 'It's not sort of learning is it? It's learning how to do things.' This comment also highlights the difference between the Amber Hill and Phoenix Park approaches. At Amber Hill, teachers tried to give the students knowledge; at Phoenix Park the students 'learned how to do things'. There was a marked contrast between the beliefs of these students and the Amber Hill students who thought that they needed to remember a vast number of rules and procedures. It was this difference in belief that may have caused the variation in the students' use of mathematics in the GCSE examination and in the applied assessments. The students at Phoenix Park were not restricted by the need to remember algorithms and procedures:

JB: How long do you think you can remember work after you've done it?
G: Well, I have an idea a long time after and I could probably go on from that, I wouldn't remember exactly how I done it, but I'd have an idea what to do.

(Gary, Phoenix Park, Year 11, MC)

Here Gary also supports a relational view of knowing, he dismissed the view that set pieces of knowledge existed in his head that he could transfer from one situation to another ('I wouldn't remember exactly how I done it') and stated that his thoughts would only be *informed* by previously held ideas, he would 'go on from that' and form new ideas of what he had to do in different situations. The students at Phoenix Park only needed to remember an idea and move on from that, which may not have been as difficult as trying to remember a complex set of algorithms and procedures. This would also fit with the superior performance of the Year 10 students using statistics over the Year 9 students trying to recall a long-division algorithm in the long-term learning tests. At Phoenix Park the students seemed to have developed the ability to think holistically about the requirements of situations, probably because they needed to do this in their projects. They were prepared to think about questions, even if they did not know, or remember, any set procedures to use. This approach will probably have contributed towards their superior performance on the conceptual questions in the examination and on applied and long-term assessments. The equivalent performance of both sets of students on procedural GCSE questions, despite the Amber Hill students' motivation, examination preparation and commitment to learning procedures, must also have been due to the willingness of the Phoenix Park students to think for themselves and work out what they needed to do in procedural questions.

Using mathematics in the 'real world'

At Amber Hill, the students reported that they did not make use of their school-learned mathematical methods, because they could not see any connections between the mathematics of the classroom and the mathematics they met in their everyday lives. At Phoenix Park, the students did not regard the mathematics they learned in school as inherently different from the mathematics of the 'real world':

JB: Can you think of a time outside school when you've had to do something mathematical ever?

T: I do sometimes when I'm at home and I have to work out like prices and stuff, that's when I use it.

JB: And is it similar or different to the way you do maths at school?

T: Similar.

L: Yes and sometimes you use it in other lessons in school, like in IT [information technology] you use it sometimes.

(Tanya and Laura, Phoenix Park, Year 10, MC)

JB: When you do something with maths in it outside of school, does it feel like when you are doing maths in school or does it feel different?

G: No, I think I can connect back to what I done in class so I know what I'm doing.

JB: What do you think?

J: It just comes naturally, once you've learned it you don't forget.

(Gavin and John, Phoenix Park, Year 10, MC)

When I asked the students at Phoenix Park the same questions as the students at Amber Hill, about their use of school-learned methods or their own methods, three-quarters of the 36 students chose their school-learned methods, this compared with none of the 40 Amber Hill students:

JB: And when you use maths in situations outside of school, do you use the methods you have learned in school or do you tend to use your own?

T: Use those maths what I've learned here.

(Tina, Phoenix Park, Year 11, RT)

A: What we've learned here probably has been helpful and I would probably look back and use that.

(Angus, Phoenix Park, Year 11, RT)

G: I'd probably try and use what I've learned in school.
I: So would I.

(Gary and Ian, Phoenix Park, Year 11, JC)

D: Probably try and think back to here and maybe try and think of my own methods sometimes, depending what sort of situation.
JB: So you would think back here for some things?
A: Yes it would be really easy to think back here.
JB: Why do you think that?
A: I dunno, I just remember a lot of stuff from here; it's not because it wasn't long ago, it's just because . . . it's just in my mind.

(Danny and Alex, Phoenix Park, Year 11, JC)

The students also reported that they made use of their school-learned mathematics in a variety of different situations:

JB: Can you think of a time when you've used maths when you've been out of school?
G: Yes.
JB: What sort of situation?
G: My job at the Co-op.
JB: And you use maths there?
G: Yes.
JB: Do you find that you can?
G: Yes, it's easy.

(Gary, Phoenix Park, Year 10, MC)

JB: Can you think of a time in your everyday lives when you've had to use something mathematical, any sort of maths?
I: I think a lot of the time you use it without noticing.

(Ian, Phoenix Park, Year 10, RT)

N: Maths is a bit like integrated humanities.
JB: Why?
N: Because we use maths things there and humanities things here.

(Nicola, Phoenix Park, Year 11, RT)

It's structured so that . . . it helps with other subjects like science, the results and drawing conclusions, it helps develop those skills.

(Alex, Phoenix Park, Year 11, JC)

Although the students at the two schools were only giving their reports of their use of mathematics, these reports were consistent with the mathematical behaviour they demonstrated in other situations. The Amber Hill students' descriptions indicated that they saw little use for the mathematics they learned in school in out-of-school situations and so, in 'real-world' mathematical situations, they abandoned their school-learned mathematics and invented their own methods. The students appeared to regard the *worlds* of the school mathematics classroom and the rest of their lives as inherently different. This was not true for the Phoenix Park students who had not constructed boundaries around their school mathematical knowledge in quite the same way (Siskin 1994). This idea will be developed further in Chapter 8, when I will aim to show that the differences between the ideas and understandings of the Amber Hill and Phoenix Park students were indicative of two different *forms* of knowledge and that these differences support an emerging perspective within the field of situated cognition.

8

Different forms of knowledge

Introduction

In this chapter, I will consider the different assessments and indications of the students' mathematical understanding that have been presented so far, provide an explanatory framework for the apparent differences between students at the two schools, Amber Hill and Phoenix Park, and use this framework to inform some of the suggested positions in the field of situated cognition. As part of this I will present a case for two different forms of mathematical knowledge. One of these forms of knowledge, I will suggest, is inert, inflexible and tied to the situation or context in which it was learned (Whitehead 1962). The other form of knowledge, I will suggest, is more adaptable, usable and relational in form (Lave 1993).

Amber Hill

Whitehead describes forms of knowledge that may only be recalled when specifically asked for as inert. Schoenfeld (1985) asserts that students develop this type of knowledge in response to conventional pedagogic practices in mathematics that demonstrate specified routines that should be learned. These practices, he suggests, cause students to develop a procedural knowledge that they can use only in standard textbook situations. In less procedural situations, students are forced to base their mathematical decision-making upon irrelevant features of questions such as the format in which they are presented or the key words used (Schoenfeld 1988). The knowledge and behaviour described by Whitehead and Schoenfeld characterized the Amber Hill students' response to different mathematical demands very well. The students had developed an inert, procedural knowledge and the reason for this seemed to be that the students had learned the teachers' methods and rules without really understanding them. This meant that in real or applied situations, the students were forced to look for cues which might indicate what they had to do.

The teachers at Amber Hill encouraged students to learn the set methods they gave them because they thought that this would make the subject clearer and easier for students. The students would not need to interpret the situations and understand what was going on as long as they could remember a procedure they had learned. When the teachers prepared the students for the examinations, they encouraged them to rehearse the rules they had taught them, rather than to think mathematically about the situations presented:

> It's different to when you read them in the book, like he told us, sir told us that in our exam we don't look at the story, we just look at the numbers.
>
> (Marco, Amber Hill, Year 11, set 4)

In the examination, and in applied assessments, students were forced to look for cues because they had no other way of knowing what to do. They were not prepared to interpret the mathematical demands of the situations and they had not learned what different procedures meant or how they might adapt them or change them if they needed to. They did not know which procedures to choose, nor whether they were effective or correct having chosen them:

> You've got to . . . just like a computer, you'll do it, but when you get the answer you won't be sure that it's right, if it's like, you'll be like – this is how we learnt it, but is this the answer? You're never certain.
>
> (Simon, Amber Hill, Year 11, set 7)

> JB: Could you do the questions?
> S: No, I couldn't, sometimes you can, but when it comes to really complicated ones you forget it and then you have to ask the teacher to go over it again and you think – 'I remember all this,' but you don't really remember what the point was.
>
> (Suzy, Amber Hill, Year 11, set 2)

Both of these comments seem important. Simon describes how he had learned procedures and even used procedures, with little or no understanding of what they meant and Suzy captures the essence of the problem: the students remembered what to do, but they did not really remember what the point was. The Cognition and Technology Group at Vanderbilt (1990) describe the ways in which different teaching approaches affect the perceptions students develop of mathematical concepts and procedures. They report that problem-oriented approaches to learning help students to view mathematical concepts as useful tools that they can use in different situations. More traditional approaches to learning cause students to view concepts 'as difficult ends to be tolerated rather than as exciting inventions (tools) that allow a variety of problems to be solved' (*ibid.* 1990: 3). Brown *et al.* (1989) draw similar distinctions between authentic and algorithmic approaches to teaching and the effect these have upon the way students view mathematical concepts and procedures. The algorithmic approach experienced by the Amber Hill students caused them to view the procedures they had learned as abstract entities, useful only for solving school textbook questions. They did not hold the view that the algorithms they had learned were exciting and useful inventions that would give them the opportunity to solve different mathematical problems.

The students' mathematical learning seemed to have created an important distinction in their minds between what they perceived as the algorithmic demands of school mathematics and the completely separate demands of the 'real world':

JB: When you use maths out of school, does it feel different to using it in school or does it feel the same?

R: Well, when I'm out of school, the maths from here is nothing to do with it to tell you the truth.

JB: What do you mean?

R: Well, it's nothing to do with this place, most of the things we've learned in school we would never use anywhere.

(Richard, Amber Hill, Year 11, set 2)

The difficulties the students experienced using mathematics in the examination and in applied assessments, combined with their reported views on the irrelevance of school-learned mathematics, make it seem unlikely that the students would make use of much of their school-learned mathematics in 'real world' situations. This is because the students had not developed a mathematical understanding which would allow them to form insights into the usefulness and appropriateness of their different methods in real situations. Indeed, the GCSE examination was probably closest in nature and demand to their textbook questions than anything else they would ever encounter, but many of the students could not relate their school-learned methods even to this. Given the students' responses to this examination, it seems hardly surprising that they abandoned their school-learned methods in the 'real world' and that they failed to perceive their relevance.

What I have tried to show here is that much of the students' learning was inert and that this derived from the students' perceptions about mathematics and, related to this, their interpretation of situations. Resnick (1993) has suggested that many sociological theories lead to the belief that the main thing people learn in school is how to behave in school. This seemed to be true for the Amber Hill students: in lessons, the students tried to interpret what to do from the cues presented in questions, and were often successful in doing so. In applied assessments, the students tried to do what was right, for example, demonstrating their knowledge of trigonometry in a question on angles, performing exact area calculations in a question on floor space. The students used the words 'angle' and 'area' as cues, rather than thinking holistically about the requirements of the questions. In the examinations, the students tried to interpret cues in a similar way, but found this to be very difficult. In none of these situations did the students think mathematically; they did not think about the situations holistically and think about the mathematics to use. This was partly because of their perceptions about mathematics and partly because the students' learning was fixed, inflexible and tied to the textbooks in which they had learned it. It is because of this that I believe they could not use it in the 'real world'. This is not to say that the students could not use mathematics outside school. As they reported, they invented their own methods in real situations and tried to work things out. But it does show that the learning they developed at school was not useful in new and different situations and the methods and procedures the students learned were of limited use. In the 'real world' and in employment situations, the students would be left to 'learn on the job':

JB: So you've been doing roofing for about a year? There's quite a lot of maths involved in that isn't there?

R: Well, when I started that I was . . . when I got there, to be honest with you I was – what? You know? It was like centimetres and inches and feet and angles and . . . like that, you know? And I was just – what? But now I pick things up as I go along.

(Richard, Amber Hill, Year 11, set 2)

Given the motivation that the students demonstrated in their mathematics lessons and their beliefs about the importance of mathematics, this total lack of preparation for the mathematical demand of the 'real world' must be considered to be unfair. The students' performance in applied assessments and their reports of their use of mathematics in different situations should also raise serious questions about the utility of their learning for anything other than working through textbooks.

Phoenix Park

The students at Phoenix Park were considerably more confident in their use of mathematics in new and real situations than the students at Amber Hill and they related this confidence to the approach of the school:

L: Yeah, when we did percentages and that, we sort of worked them out as though we were out of school using them.

V: And most of the activities we did you could use.

L: Yeah, most of the activities you'd use – not the actual same things as the activities, but things you could use them in.

(Lindsey and Vicky, Phoenix Park, Year 11, JC)

The students gave indications that the mathematics they learned through their project-based work was useful in new and different situations. This seemed to derive from a way of thinking and working in which the students learned to adapt and change methods to fit the demands of different situations. This again supports a situated view of learning (Lave 1993), because the students described the ways in which they developed meaning in interaction with different settings. Lindsey said that she would use mathematics 'not the actual same things as the activities, but things you could use them in'; she would adapt and transform what she had learned to fit new situations. Later in the interview she said:

L: Well if you find a rule or a method, you try and adapt it to other things; when we found this rule that worked with the circles we started to work out the percentages and then adapted it, so we just took it further and took different steps and tried to adapt it to new situations.

(Lindsey, Phoenix Park, Year 11, JC)

The analysis offered by Lindsey in this extract is very important, for it was this willingness to adapt and change methods to fit new situations which seemed to underlie the students' confidence in their use of mathematics in 'real world' situations. Indeed, many of the students' descriptions suggest that they had learned mathematics in a way that transcended the boundaries (Lave 1996a) which generally exist between the classroom and real situations.

> J: Solve the problems and think about other problems and solve them, problems that aren't connected with maths, think about them.
> JB: You think the way you do maths helps you to do that?
> J: Yes.
> JB: Things that aren't to do with maths?
> J: It's more the thinking side to sort of look at everything you've got and think about how to solve it.
>
> (Jackie, Phoenix Park, Year 10, JC)

The idea that students may have developed a usable form of mathematics in response to their project work was partly supported by the students' views about the nature of their bookwork. When they described the mathematics they learned in SMP books at middle school, the mathematics they learned through their projects at Phoenix Park and the examination revision of Year 11, the contrast they offered between the three approaches centred around the adaptability of their learning:

> JB: Do you think you learn different things – doing activities and working from a book?
> L: I think you tend to understand it more when you do it with the activities.
> V: 'Cause you're trying to work it out.
> L: Yeah, and you understand how they got it, when you're working from a book; you just know that's the thing and that you just stick to it; you tend to understand it more from the activities.
>
> (Lindsey and Vicky, Phoenix Park, Year 11, JC)

> JB: If you were in a job situation or something outside of school and there was something mathematical you had to do, do you think you would think back to things you'd learned here and use that?
> L: I wouldn't be able to use the stuff now because I don't understand it [examination preparation].
> H: No, we only understand it as in the way how, what it's been set, like this is a fraction, so alright then.
> L: But, like Pope's theory I'll always remember – when you had to draw something I'll always remember the, like the projects we used to do.
> H: Yeah, they were helpful for things you would use later, the projects.
>
> (Linda and Helen, Phoenix Park, Year 11, MC)

When Helen says that 'we only understand it as in the way how, what it's been set' she seems to be describing the inflexible nature of her learning, but she contrasts this with her project work which she regarded as 'helpful for things you would use later'. Lindsey also seems to be describing the implicit boundaries which surround bookwork when she says 'you just know that's the thing and that you just stick to it' and Helen talks in similar terms ('like this is a fraction, so alright then'). As part of the Phoenix Park examination preparation, the students were introduced to rules and procedures. They, like the Amber Hill students, regarded these rules as 'set' and unchangeable. These descriptions contrast with Lindsey's earlier statement about project work: 'Well if you find a rule or a method, you try and adapt it to other things.'

There were a number of indications that the students at Phoenix Park had developed a predisposition to think about and use mathematics in new and different situations and this seemed to relate to a general mathematical empowerment. This empowerment meant that they were flexible in their approach and they were prepared to take what they had learned and adapt it to fit new situations. This flexibility seemed to rest upon two important principles. First, the students had the belief that the mathematics they learned was adaptable. Many researchers have shown the rigid and inflexible models of mathematics that students develop which stop them from using mathematics in new situations (Schoenfeld 1985; Brown *et al.* 1989; Young 1993). The comments given by Phoenix Park students in Chapter 5 demonstrated that they viewed mathematics as an active, exploratory and adaptable subject. The second important feature of their learning was the ability they appeared to have developed to adapt and change methods and to think mathematically.

T: Yes, when I go shopping I just . . . get all the things in the basket, number them all at a pound, for example if some of them are 50p and some of them are £2, I just call them all a pound and see how much I've got in my pocket, then hope for the best. It usually gets me . . . it's worked every time actually.

JB: That's not a bad strategy if some of the prices are more and some less.

T: Yes, you've just got to make sure that there's more that are less than a pound than more than a pound or else you haven't got enough money.

(Trevor, Phoenix Park, Year 11, RT)

Trevor was not describing any complex mathematical thinking in this extract, but his description was interesting for two reasons. First, Trevor chose this situation as an example of the way he used his school-learned mathematics in the 'real world'; second, his statement demonstrates the confidence he had to think mathematically in a 'real' situation. The students were very clear in interviews about the source of their mathematical confidence. This they related to two features of their approach. The first was the fact that they had been forced to become autonomous learners. The second, which was related to this, was the fact that they had always been encouraged to think for themselves:

N: You had to be self-motivated.

JB: Is that fair do you think?

N: Well, it was good for us because it taught us to do things by ourselves so it made you confident to do things for yourself.

(Nicola, Phoenix Park, Year 11, RT)

JB: Did doing the project work help you in any way do you think?

T: Yes, thinking for yourself and motivating yourself I think.

(Tina, Phoenix Park, Year 11, RT)

S: At the start of Year 9, the teacher told you what to do and explained all the skills and you just did it and then gradually you begin to think more for yourself – you know – what shall I do next? What shall I do about this?

(Simon, Phoenix Park, Year 11, JC)

The students contrasted their experiences of project work and book work by saying that project work required them to work things out and think, whilst bookwork or boardwork did not:

T: I think it allows, when you first come to the school you do your projects and it allows you to think more for yourself than when you were in middle school and you worked from the board or from books, things like that.

(Tina, Phoenix Park, Year 11, RT)

A: With the SMP books it just sort of . . . say you were doing the SMP books on percentages or something, it would just ask you a series of questions on it, like find the percentages of this and that, but if you did an investigation on it, you would have to, like, think a lot more about it for yourself and how to like solve the problem. I would say it's a lot more interesting than doing SMP books.

(Angus, Phoenix Park, Year 11, RT)

This requirement to think in mathematics lessons was central to Phoenix Park's approach. The students were given very little structure and guidance and although many spent long periods of time off task, when they were working, they needed to be thinking. It was almost impossible for the students to switch off and work in a procedural way when they were planning and developing their projects. For some students this was the most important difference between their bookwork and project work:

G: In books it more or less explains everything to it, but I'd rather work it out by myself by looking at it and working it out or getting the teacher to talk to you about it, instead of telling you exactly what to do.

I: And in the books you don't understand it.

G: And you take it in if you've done it but if you read it, you just read it and you don't take any notice.

(Gary and Ian, Phoenix Park, Year 11, JC)

H: The stuff we're doing now [examination preparation], it's more fractions and figures.

L: Like, we'll do a lesson or something and some of us don't understand it and then next lesson we'll do something completely different; that's harder and you can't remember anything.

JB: So what's different?

L: We were using them before, but now we're just writing them.

H: And vaguely understanding them and having a little bit of discussion and thinking, 'Oh I don't understand that' or 'I understand this, and then you just leave it, but I'd say some of the work we did before we do use now or out of school or whatever.

(Helen and Linda, Phoenix Park, Year 11, MC)

The difference for Linda, between bookwork and project work was, 'We were using them before, but now we're just writing them.' Gary drew out a similar distinction saying, 'You take it in if you've done it but if you read it, you just read it.' Helen chose to say, without prompting or asking, that she used the mathematics she learned through the projects 'now or out of school or whatever'. Perhaps the most important distinction of all, between bookwork and project work, was provided by Sue:

JB: Do you think when you use maths outside of school, it feels very different to using maths in school, or does it feel similar?

S: Very different from what we do now, if we do use maths outside of school it's got the same atmosphere as how it used to be, but not now.

JB: What do you mean by – 'it's got the same atmosphere'?

S: Well, when we used to do projects, it was like that, looking at things and working them out, solving them – so it was similar to that, but it's not similar to this stuff now, it's, you don't know what this stuff is for really, except the exam.

(Sue, Phoenix Park, Year 11, MC)

Sue, was particularly lucid in her comparison of the two approaches: one was about solving problems, 'looking at things and working them out, solving them', the other did not hold any meaning for her – 'you don't know what this stuff is for really, except the exam'. Sue, like other students, distinguished between the two approaches in terms of the usefulness of the mathematics she had learned. One version was similar to the mathematics of the 'real world', the other was not.

Situated cognition

The relative underachievement of the students at Amber Hill in formal test situations may be considered surprising, partly because the students worked hard in mathematics lessons and partly because the school's mathematical approach was extremely examination-oriented. However, after many hours of watching the students work at Amber Hill and talking to the students in interviews I was not surprised by the relative performance of the two sets of students. This was because the learning of the Amber Hill students was extremely inflexible and inert and although many were able to use their mathematical methods within textbook questions, when the demands of situations were only slightly different to the ones they were used to, they failed. They had developed a knowledge that appeared to be effective only in other textbook or similar situations.

I would relate this problem to three aspects of their learning. First, they were not encouraged to think about or understand the methods they used in class, so they were not able to consider the methods they had learned and make informed decisions about the ones they should use. Second, they believed that mathematics was about remembering methods, rather than thinking about questions. In class, they had all been taught to learn methods and to practise them, not to adapt them or think about them. The third problem seemed to be caused by the students' perceptions of the mathematics classroom as a distinct 'community of practice' (Lave 1993, 1996a) in which mathematical rules and procedures were learned that were specific to that community of practice.

At Phoenix Park, the students were probably less motivated to do well in examinations. They spent less time on task in lessons, they had not been introduced to all of the content and procedures they needed in the examination and they were not even given the necessary equipment for the examination. But the students were more successful in the examination, and in applied and long-term assessments, apparently because they had developed a different *form* of learning. The nature and form of this learning is interesting to consider, particularly in the light of new developments in the field of situated cognition which have gone some way towards outlining the qualities of learning that enhance or inhibit its usefulness.

Gibson (1986) is cited as providing the most extreme position on situated learning (Young 1993). Gibson asserts that when individuals develop meaning from situations, they do so through a process of 'perceiving and acting' and by creating meaning on the spot, rather than by using their memory of representations stored in the head (Gibson 1986: 258). Young suggests that, in Gibson's theory 'the concept of memory becomes non-existent or irrelevant to an explanation of knowing and learning, replaced by an emphasis of the tuning of attention and perception' (Young 1993: 44). There is some debate as to whether Gibson replaced or just repositioned the importance of memory (Greeno *et al.* 1993) but the students' descriptions of their learning at Phoenix Park suggest that their success in new situations was due to their ability to perceive and interpret what was needed from situations *combined with* their ability to adapt and make use of procedures they remembered. From this perspective, perception and interpretation of situations becomes the *key* to effective learning, partly because this development of meaning enabled the students to reflect upon prior experience. For whilst I agree with Gibson's suggestion that meaning is generated 'on the spot', I would suggest that the way in which this was made possible for the Phoenix Park students was that their thought and interpretation enabled their memory of the mathematics they had used before to be enacted.

Lave (1996a) asserts that students do not use mathematics learned in one situation in another situation because the two situations represent different 'communities of practice'. The students relate to them differently and form different ideas in relation to the two settings. This analysis is similar to one offered by Bernstein in which he suggests that educational knowledge is 'uncommonsense knowledge' (1971: 58) and that children are socialized early in their lives into knowledge frames which discourage connections with everyday realities. Lave (1996b) asserts that when students do use mathematics developed in one setting in another setting, it is because they have perceived and interpreted the settings in a similar way and formed similar representations and meanings in the two settings. This view appears to be consonant with the views of the Phoenix Park students. When the Phoenix Park students reported their successful use of mathematics, they focused upon the way that they thought about mathematics in different situations, interpreted what was needed and formed ideas in relation to their setting. They refuted the idea that they had used knowledge learned at school in the same form elsewhere.

Lave (1988, 1996a) proposes that transfer is an impoverished and inadequate concept that cannot explain the way individuals act in different settings. She, and others in the field of situated cognition, have suggested that knowledge should be represented as an interpretation of experience and that distinctions should not be drawn between knowledge and the way people perform in different settings. In this view, knowledge is constructed in different situations; it is not transferred from one situation to another and it is not regarded 'as a process of taking a given item and applying it somewhere else' (Lave 1988: 37). The Phoenix Park students seemed to add support to this notion because they indicated that they were not transferring knowledge but constructing it in relation to the situation they were in. Lave proposes that notions of knowing should be replaced with notions of doing and the Phoenix Park students seem to have developed a similar view:

> It's not sort of learning is it? It's learning how to do things.
>
> (Philip, Phoenix Park, Year 11, JC)

The ability of the Phoenix Park students to use mathematics in different situations can be taken as some support for the use of 'cognitive apprenticeship' approaches in classrooms. Such approaches (see, for example, the Jasper series, developed by the Cognition and Technology group at Vanderbilt 1990) involve presenting students with realistic problems which require them to learn new concepts and ideas in order to solve the problems. This research supports such approaches because the reason the students seemed able to use their mathematics at Phoenix Park was not because they had learned it in a clear and straightforward way, but because they had used mathematics in a similar way in the classroom. They had been *apprenticed* into this type of mathematical use. As Sue said, when they used mathematics outside school, it felt the same, it 'had the same atmosphere' as their project-based mathematics. Even the vast differences between the nature of Phoenix Park's open-ended projects and the GCSE examination did not faze the students. This was because they did not regard the two assessments as inherently different:

> JB: Did the questions in the exam seem similar to what you'd done in class or did they seem different?
>
> L: Most of them seemed similar didn't they?
>
> JB: The exam was similar to your project work?
>
> L: Most of it seemed the same really.
>
> (Louise, Phoenix Park, Year 11, JC)

Within school the Phoenix Park students did not view mathematics as a formalized and abstract entity that was useful only for school mathematics problems. They had not constructed 'boundaries' (Siskin 1994) around their school mathematical understandings in the way that the Amber Hill students had. At Amber Hill, the students developed a narrow view of mathematics that they regarded as useful only within classroom textbook situations. The students regarded the school mathematics classroom as one 'community of practice' (Lave 1993, 1996a) and other places, even the school examination hall, as different communities of practice.

Lave (1996a) claims that learning would be enhanced if we were to consider and understand how barriers are generated that make individuals view the worlds of school and the rest of their lives as different communities of practice. At Amber Hill there were strong institutional barriers which separated the students' experiences of school from their experiences of the rest of the world. Many of these barriers were constituents of Bernstein's visible pedagogy (Bernstein 1975). General school rules and practices such as school uniform, timetables, discipline and order contributed to these as well as the esoteric mathematical practices of formalization and rule-following. At Phoenix Park, the barriers between school and the real world were less distinct: there were no bells at the school, students did not wear uniform, the teachers did not give them orders, they could make choices about the nature and organization of their work and whether they worked or not, mathematics was not presented as a formalized, algorithmic subject and the mathematics classroom was a social arena. The communities of practice making up school and the real world were not inherently different. From this perspective, the Phoenix Park students were more able to make use of their school-learned mathematics because they had been enculturated into a practice of thinking, talking, representing and interpreting in the classroom. The students' knowledge of mathematical procedures at the two schools may have been similar but the way they connected and interacted with mathematics and formed mathematical relations was different, because of the way that they had been enculturated or apprenticed at school.

It was the perceiving and interpreting of situations that seemed to characterize the main difference between the students at the two schools. When the students were presented with the angle problem in the 'Architectural' task (pp. 65–8), many of the Amber Hill students were unsuccessful, not because they were not capable of estimating an angle, but because they could not interpret the situation. Similarly, in the 'Planning a flat' activity (pp. 68–72), 25 Amber Hill students could not work out the area of their flat, not because they were incapable of calculating areas, but because they did not interpret what was needed in the situation. The Phoenix Park students, on the other hand, were not as well versed in mathematical procedures, but they were able to interpret and develop meaning in the situations they encountered. The fact that the Amber Hill students had learned more procedures than the Phoenix Park students demonstrates the inadequacy of transfer theories in explaining individuals' use or non-use of subject matter. This is because the Amber Hill students' non-use of mathematics had nothing to do with the knowledge of procedures they did or did not own – the students could reproduce relevant procedures in *certain* contexts. Similarly, the Phoenix Park students effective use of mathematics must be taken as a support for a relational view of learning, because it was the students' ability or predisposition to think and form meaning in different settings that differentiated them from the Amber Hill students.

Of course, it is not the case that *all* the Amber Hill students had developed a shallow, procedural knowledge, and *all* the Phoenix Park students were able to use mathematics effectively. At Phoenix Park some of the students persisted in the belief that they needed to learn set rules and methods in order to be successful mathematicians. Others took to the open approach and flourished within it. I have not found it possible to find out why different students responded to the Phoenix Park approach in different ways, but it is not surprising that some students resisted the open nature of the mathematics when they had learned mathematics in a very different way for eight years prior to attending Phoenix Park and they were only at Phoenix Park for three years. Similarly, at Amber Hill, some students developed an effective mathematical understanding, because they were able to look beyond what they were given and make their own sense of the different methods they encountered. The two approaches are not, therefore, at opposite ends of a spectrum of mathematical effectiveness, but the differences between the approaches do serve to illuminate the potential of the different methods of teaching for the development of different *forms* of knowledge.

Conclusions

The data presented in this chapter and in Chapter 6 lead to a number of possible conclusions that I have set out below:

1 When students are taught mathematical procedures, but they are not encouraged to locate these within wider mathematical perspectives, they can only develop a 'procedural' knowledge (Schoenfeld 1985; Hiebert 1986) and this knowledge is extremely limited in its applicability (Boaler, 1998). The lack of understanding that the Amber Hill students had of the different methods they used in class also meant that they found it very difficult remembering methods and using them, even in textbook questions, a few weeks after their original textbook lessons. The students often got by in lessons by interpreting SMP cues (Schoenfeld 1985), but they found that similar cues were not present within authentic tasks, conceptual GCSE questions or non-school situations.

2 The absence of set procedures and algorithms from the Phoenix Park students' knowledge may have given them the freedom to interpret situations and develop meaning from them. It could be that it was the Amber Hill students' knowledge of rules and algorithms that inhibited their ability to interpret the different situations they encountered. This is a tentative suggestion, but it is supported by a research study conducted by Perry (1991). In this experimental study, Perry compared principle-based and procedure-based instruction. This showed that the two types of instruction led a comparable number of children to learn mathematical concepts, but the principle-based instruction led significantly more students to 'transfer' their

knowledge to new situations. Perry then repeated the study with an additional type of instruction which combined principles and procedures. In this instruction, students were given procedures to learn, but they were also taught about the principles behind them. These students performed in a virtually identical way to the procedure-only students. Perry concluded from this that, when students were exposed to procedures, they ignored the 'conceptually rich information inherent in the principles' (Perry 1991: 449). This, and some of the students' responses at the two schools, could suggest that the Phoenix Park students' ability to interpret different situations was enhanced because of their lack of knowledge of standard mathematical rules and algorithms. These may have served as barriers or boundaries (Bernstein 1971; Siskin 1994) for the Amber Hill students which contributed towards the formation of distinct communities of practice (Lave 1993, 1996a).

3 The largely procedural nature of the mathematics GCSE examination and the requirement of teachers to prepare students for this examination may have detracted from the Phoenix Park students' mathematical understanding. This is also a tentative suggestion, based upon the Phoenix Park students' responses to their examination preparation. The Phoenix Park students, like the Amber Hill students, reported that they were confused by the different 'rules and equations' they were introduced to and, like the Amber Hill students, they could not see their relevance for anything other than the examination. Chapter 5 also demonstrated that the students' examination preparation had caused them to narrow their views of mathematics.

4 The use of cognitive apprenticeship approaches in classrooms has represented an interesting development and early indications are that these 'realistic' approaches to learning (Cognition and Technology Group at Vanderbilt 1990) are successful. The students' mathematical capabilities and perceptions at Amber Hill and Phoenix Park seem to add further support to some of the features of classroom cognitive apprenticeship, such as authenticity and the need to use mathematics. This is because the introduction of mathematical ideas as part of meaningful activities seemed to enable the Phoenix Park students to develop an inherent understanding of the meaning of the procedures they encountered. The students formed a belief in the utility of the mathematical procedures they used and they learned to regard them as adaptable and flexible. They experienced mathematics on many different levels (Lave 1996a) and they learned to interpret situations and develop mathematical ideas in relation to a range of different settings. The understandings and perceptions that resulted from this apprenticeship or enculturation seemed to lead to an increased competence in new and unfamiliar situations. This appeared to derive from:

- a willingness and ability to perceive and interpret different situations and develop meaning from them (Gibson 1986), and in relation to them (Lave 1993, 1996a);
- a sufficient understanding of different procedures to allow appropriate procedures to be drawn upon (Whitehead 1962); and
- a mathematical confidence and understanding that led students to adapt and change procedures to fit the demands of new situations.

The Amber Hill students were not given the opportunity to interpret different situations, to form knowledge in relation to different settings or to think about or reflect upon different procedures. They did not use mathematics within authentic activities or discuss mathematics in a social environment. All these features seem to have been important to the Phoenix Park students and all these features were present in Phoenix Park's project approach and completely absent in Amber Hill's textbook approach.

The results of this study lend support to some of the emerging ideas within the field of situated cognition. For example, the results have demonstrated the relational nature of learning and the interdependency of person, activity, knowledge and setting (Lave 1993). The results have also shown that attempts to impart knowledge to students are less helpful than classroom environments in which students are enculturated and apprenticed into a system of knowing, thinking and doing.

9

Girls, boys and learning styles

Introduction

> Perhaps we don't take seriously enough the voices that say again and again, 'but it doesn't make sense', and 'what's the point of it?' Perhaps what they are saying simply is true. Perhaps mathematics, their mathematics, secondary-school mathematics, doesn't make sense. Perhaps the fault is in the mathematics, and not the teaching, not the learning, not the people. At the very least it is a question worth focusing on for a while.
>
> (Johnston 1995: 225)

Johnston presents an important idea in this extract that I intend to explore and develop in this chapter. Many of the Amber Hill students experienced a mathematics that did make little sense to them and although both girls and boys were negatively affected by this, the greatest disadvantages were experienced by the girls, mainly because of their preferred learning styles and ways of working. In this chapter I shall examine the different responses of the girls and boys at the two schools. In doing so, I will extend theoretical positions about the learning styles of girls and boys and the potential of different approaches for equity (see also Boaler 1997b). I will also illuminate further the different learning experiences of the students at Amber Hill and Phoenix Park and the effect that these had upon their understanding of mathematics.

The underachievement and non-participation of girls in mathematics has become an established focus of concern over recent years. As a result of this, many feminists and others with equity concerns, have developed a range of initiatives which have been successful at raising girls' achievement, if not their continued participation. At GCSE, girls now attain the same proportion of 'good' grades as boys (i.e. A*–C) and stereotyped attitudes about the irrelevance of mathematics for girls are largely disappearing. However, important differences still occur amongst the top 5 per cent of students. In 1993, approximately five boys to every four girls attained a GCSE grade A and girls made up only 35 per cent of the 1995 A-level cohort. One of the consistent themes that has emerged from the literature on gender differences has concerned open, problem-solving environments. These have been claimed to produce equity amongst students (Burton 1995; Rogers and Kaiser 1995), although there has been little research evidence available to support such claims. Official sources such as Her Majesty's Inspectorate (1985) and Cockcroft (1982) in the UK and the National Council for Teachers of Mathematics (1989) in the United States have also made proposals to further the use of open-ended work in order to improve the mathematical experiences of boys and girls. Where feminist researchers have diverged from the more general reformists is in their claim that school mathematics has traditionally disadvantaged girls, because of the ways girls tend to think and work and the ways that they come to *know*.

Becker (1995) and Belencky *et al.* (1986) both take Gilligan's notion of 'separate' and 'connected' to suggest that women and men have differential preferences for ways of knowing and subsequent ways of working. Thus women tend to value 'connected' knowledge which involves intuition, creativity and experience, whilst men tend to value 'separate' knowledge which is characterized by logic, rigour and abstraction. Becker (1995) claims that girls have traditionally been denied access to success in mathematics because they tend to be 'connected' thinkers, and traditional models of mathematics teaching have encouraged 'separate' ways of working. Head (1995) has suggested that girls also prefer co-operative, supportive working environments whereas boys work well in competitive, pressurized environments. These various claims about the gendered preferences of students seem important to consider in the light of the girls' and boys' responses to mathematics teaching at Amber Hill and Phoenix Park. This is because the Phoenix Park approach presented an open, discursive and experiential form of mathematics, that enabled both 'separate' and 'connected' thinking, and the responses of girls to this, and the traditional approach of Amber Hill, inform the new theoretical positions proposed. The perspectives of the students at Amber Hill and Phoenix Park are also made important by the fact that there is very little research available to support the claims made about the potential of process-based mathematical environments, mainly because of the scarcity of these environments in schools.

Amber Hill school

Throughout my research study many of the girls *and* boys at Amber Hill expressed strong preferences for their 'coursework' lessons and spoke vividly about their dislike of textbook lessons. However, the reasons the girls and boys gave for their preferences and, importantly, the responses of the students to the textbook approach they disliked, were qualitatively different. This difference was intricate and complex but for the girls it involved what I would call a 'quest for understanding'; for the boys it involved playing a kind of school mathematics *game*. I will attempt to illustrate and illuminate these propositions now.

The quest for understanding

All of the Amber Hill girls interviewed in Years 10 and 11 expressed a strong preference for their course-work lessons and for the individualized booklet approach which they followed in Years 7 and 8, as against their textbook work. The girls gave very clear reasons why these two approaches were more appropriate ways of learning mathematics for them; all of these reasons were linked to their desire to understand mathematics. In conversations and interviews, students expressed a concern for their lack of understanding of the mathematics they encountered in class. This was particularly acute for the girls, not because they understood less than the boys, but because they appeared to be less willing to relinquish their desire for understanding:

> J: He'll write it on the board and you end up thinking, well how comes this and this? How did you get that answer? Why did you do that?, but . . .
>
> M: You don't really know because he's gone through it on the board so fast and . . .
>
> J: Because he understands it he thinks we all do and we don't.
>
> (Jane and Mary, Amber Hill, Year 11, set 1)

These students show that they were interested in meaning and understanding. They did not just want to learn work, they wanted to know 'how comes this and this?, how did you get that answer?' Many of the boys did not like their textbook lessons and they did not understand any more of the work than the girls, but they seemed to have formed different goals to the girls. These related to speed and the attainment of correct answers, rather than understanding. Thus, typically:

> I don't mind working out of textbooks, because you can get ahead of everyone else.
>
> (Alan, Amber Hill, Year 11, set 3)

> I dunno; the only maths lessons you like are when you've really done a lot of work and you're proud of yourself because you've done so much work, you're so much ahead of everyone else.
>
> (James, Amber Hill, Year 10, set 2)

Both of these boys emphasized the importance of *relative* performance (Head 1995), rather than absolute learning. The goals and expectations of many of the boys related to working quickly and completing lots of questions. These were not particularly beneficial goals, in the long term, for the boys came to regard mathematics as a system of rule-following and rote learning. However, as a coping strategy, the boys' response was more productive in accommodating to the demands of the school system. Many of the girls were very concerned about understanding their mathematics and because they felt they were unable to do so, they would often become anxious and fall behind.

> When I understand there's no stopping me, you saw me with that, when we had that equation sheet and the end of the lesson came and I was – 'Do we have to go? I just want to finish this.' Once I understand something I'm alright, but it kind of frustrates me if I'm sitting there for an hour and I don't know exactly what I'm doing.
>
> (Jane, Amber Hill, Year 11, set 1)

The only work I like is when I understand what I'm doing; it's when I don't understand and I get confused, that's when I don't like it much.

(Mary, Amber Hill, Year 11, set 1)

As a result of a number of different data sources, I became convinced that it was this desire to understand, rather than any difference in understanding, that really differentiated the girls from the boys. The girls knew that they needed to understand mathematics, but they felt that they had limited access to understanding within their fast, pressured, textbook system.

I just try and do it now, I don't know what it means, I just try and work fast.

(Sara, Amber Hill, Year 10, set 3)

The girls' preference for understanding caused them to become disaffected in relation to mathematics. For some girls this disaffection was heightened by their awareness of the mismatch between their desire for understanding and their classroom experiences:

JB: Is maths more about understanding work or remembering it?
J: More understanding, if you understand it you're bound to remember it.
L: Yeah, but the way sir teaches, it's like he just wants us to remember it, when you don't really understand things.

(Jackie and Louise, Amber Hill, Year 10, set 1)

Further evidence of the different priorities held by the girls and boys at Amber Hill came from questionnaires. In their Year 10 questionnaire, I asked the students to rank five different areas of mathematics in terms of their importance. These were: getting a lot of work done; working at a fast pace; understanding; remembering rules and methods; and knowing how to use a calculator. Three of these categories produced significant differences between girls and boys at Amber Hill:

- 91 per cent of girls regarded 'understanding' as the most important aspect of learning mathematics, compared with 65 per cent of boys.
- 4 per cent of girls regarded 'remembering rules and methods' as the most important, compared with 24 per cent of boys.
- 5 per cent of girls regarded 'getting a lot of work done' as the most or second most important aspect of learning mathematics, compared with 19 per cent of boys.

The differential responses of girls and boys were also evident in lessons. During my lesson observations, I would frequently observe boys racing through their textbook questions, trying to work as quickly as possible and complete as many questions as they could. I would, just as frequently, observe girls looking lost and confused, struggling to understand their work or giving up all together. In lessons I would often ask students to explain what they were doing. The vast majority of the time the students would tell me the chapter title and, if I asked them questions like, 'Yes, but what are you actually *doing*?' They would tell me the number in the exercise; neither girls nor boys would be able to tell me why they were using methods or what they meant. On the whole, the boys seemed unconcerned, or less concerned, by this, as long as they were getting their questions right. The girls would get questions right, but they wanted more:

> It's like, you have to work it out and you get the right answers but you don't know what you did, you don't know how you got them, you know?
> (Marsha, Amber Hill, Year 10, set 4)

Marsha, like Jane and Mary earlier, demonstrates a desire for understanding and meaning which extends beyond the acquisition of 'right answers'.

Positive learning experiences

The girls at Amber Hill were not only critical of their school's mathematical methods and in interviews they offered extremely clear descriptions of positive learning experiences. All of these experiences took place during coursework lessons or individualized booklet lessons. The reasons that the girls liked these approaches were related to the freedom they experienced to use their own ideas, work as a group or work at their own pace. All these practices, the girls claimed, gave them access to a depth of understanding that textbook work denied them.

In Chapter 4, I described the preferences the students had for open-ended work. This was generally because the students did not believe that their textbook lessons allowed them to use their own ideas or think creatively. Preferences for these features of their learning, features that allowed a 'connected' way of working (Gilligan 1982, Becker 1995), were more prevalent amongst girls than boys. This was shown by some of the Year 11 questionnaire responses that prompted significant differences between girls and boys. Significantly more boys agreed with the following:

- It is important in maths to answer questions the way the teacher wants you to (girls = 49 per cent, boys = 70 per cent).

Whereas significantly more girls agreed with the statements:

- It is important in maths to find your own way of solving problems (girls = 84 per cent, boys = 66 per cent).
- It is important in maths to think about different types of maths (girls = 87 per cent, boys = 71 per cent).

These responses seem important because larger proportions of girls were expressing preferences for a freedom of approach and a way of working that they rarely experienced in their mathematics classrooms.

Both boys and girls at Amber Hill reported enjoying their open-ended coursework, but the boys were less convinced of the value of having to think for themselves and the need to put effort into their work, mainly because this conflicted with their desire for speed and correct answers:

> G: I don't really like investigations.
> JB: Why not?

> *G:* It's hard.
>
> *JB:* How are they different to what you do normally?
>
> *G:* Because in chapters, the teacher explains how to do it, but with the investigations you have to do it by yourself.
>
> *JB:* Is that more difficult?
>
> *G:* Yeah, 'cause in the chapters, once you know how to do it, you're away.
>
> (Gary, Amber Hill, Year 11, set 3)

Although many of the boys reported enjoying their coursework, this would generally be because it was a change, few of the boys talked about the opportunity to think or to use their initiative, or the access it gave them to understanding, whereas this was central to the reasoning of the girls.

The girls at Amber Hill also expressed preferences for working co-operatively in groups, but again the reason for this was the access that discussion and group work gave them to depth of understanding. The boys rarely mentioned their experiences of group work and those that did differed in their responses to it. Some of the boys disliked working in groups because they felt that it slowed them down:

> Well, it could have been useful, but you could do it in half the time yourself, like you speed along, you understand it, next topic. But it slows you down, the rest of the class.
>
> (Leigh, Amber Hill, Year 10, set 2)

The different responses of the girls and boys to group work related to the opportunity it gave them to think about topics in depth and to increase their understanding through discussion. This was not perceived as a great advantage to the boys, probably because the aim, for many of the boys, was not to understand, but to get through work quickly. These different responses were also evident in response to the students' preferences for working at their own pace. In Chapter 6 I showed that an overwhelming desire for both girls and boys at Amber Hill was to work at their own pace. This desire united the sexes, but the underlying reasons for this divided them. The boys enjoyed individualized work that could be completed at their own pace because it allowed them to tear ahead and complete as many books as possible:

> *C:* It was better then weren't it?
>
> *M:* Yes.
>
> *C:* We used to compete.
>
> *M:* Yeah, we could do it at our own pace.
>
> *C:* Yeah, we could do it at our own pace and we used to be books ahead of the others.
>
> (Chris and Marco, Amber Hill, Year 11, set 4)

> Before, when we had the little books, they were only short pages and we used to, like, compete with each other, see who'd done the most, who'd got the most percentage and that was, like, most interesting.
>
> (Alan, Amber Hill, Year 11, set 3)

The girls wanted to work at their own pace so that they could understand what they were doing, before they moved onto something else:

L: We had time to read it didn't we? We had time to read it through and if we didn't get it we had time to read it again, but like with this, we can only read it through once because she wants us to hurry up and get on and finish it.

(Lindsey, Amber Hill, Year 11, set 4)

The girls, again, explained their preference for working at their own pace, in terms of an increased access to understanding. The girls at Amber Hill consistently demonstrated that they believed in the importance of an open, reflective style of learning and that they did not value a competitive approach or an approach in which there was one teacher-determined answer. Unfortunately for them, the approach that they thought would enhance their understanding was not attainable in their mathematics classrooms, except for three weeks of each year.

Top set girls

In Chapter 4, I described the speed and pressure which were an important part of the set 1 experience at Amber Hill. Many of the students reported that these features of their set 1 lessons had a negative effect upon their learning and this effect seemed to be particularly detrimental for the girls. In the top set group in my case study cohort ($n = 33$), I identified 15 students who were underachieving. This identification derived from a comparison of their NFER scores for mathematics on entry to the school and their success in Years 7 and 8 when they used SMP booklets with their relative positions in the set 1 group, my assessment exercises, their GCSE grades and the opinion of their teacher. Eleven of the 15 students were girls, which represented over two-thirds of the girls in the group. In the short 'context' questions given to students at the beginning of Year 9 and again at the end of Year 10, nine of these 15 students attained *lower* grades in Year 10 than in Year 9, whereas the rest of the top set improved their grades or stayed at the same level. Most of the 15 students were easy to locate in lessons. Six of the girls sat together and looked lost, confused and unhappy in lessons and completed hardly any work. Some of these girls were, at one time, the highest mathematical attainers in the school. On entry to the school, Carly attained the highest NFER entry mark in the school and Lorna attained the second highest mark; both of these girls attained the *lowest* GCSE grade in set 1, grade E. In the Year 10 questionnaires, when students were asked to describe lessons, Carly and Lorna gave the following descriptions:

Not interesting. You go through the work too quickly and things don't get explained properly.

(Carly, Amber Hill, Year 10, set 1)

The teacher stands by the blackboard for half the lesson explaining the work and everyone seems confused and not understanding the work. It goes too fast and it is very uninteresting.

(Lorna, Amber Hill, Year 10, set 1)

In the top set there were 16 girls and 17 boys. In GCSE examinations there were significant differences between the achievement of the girls and boys in set 1, even amongst such a small number of students. In the GCSE examinations, boys attained 14 of the 19 A–C grades from set 1; girls attained 11 of the 14 D and E grades. Gender differences in achievement were most marked amongst the highest attaining students in the school, which is consistent with national patterns of mathematics performance. Such differences, although they affect a small proportion of girls, are extremely important because these high-attaining girls, who could and should be getting high grades are the students who could be future role models, such as mathematicians, engineers and teachers of mathematics. The girls are also being denied access to a subject that they could excel at:

C: When we first came to this school I had always had really high marks for maths; now I've just gone downhill.
JB: Do you know why that is?
C: I feel rushed; some areas, I don't understand, he just rushes through and I still don't understand it.

(Carly, Amber Hill, Year 11, set 1)

The experiences and attitudes of the 'high-ability' girls in the top set at Amber Hill give some indication of the possible reasons for the gender imbalance reported at the highest levels in mathematics. These may be linked to intrinsic features of the top set environments in which the majority of 'high-ability' girls work in the UK, particularly intense pressure and fast-paced lessons. Further evidence for this suggestion is provided by the work of Dweck (1986). Through a review of different research studies from the social-cognitive framework, Dweck has shown that 'maladaptive' motivational patterns affect motivation and influence the quality of performance. She has also shown that tendencies toward unduly low expectancies, challenge avoidance, ability attributions for failure and debilitation under failure have been especially noted in girls, and particularly 'bright' girls.

Dweck asserts that one of the characteristics of 'maladaptive' motivational patterns is a tendency to seek situations which will lead to good performance, rather than situations which will involve challenge and in which students may learn. But I would question whether such tendencies can really be described as 'maladaptive' in many of the mathematics classrooms in which the girls are learning. In classrooms such as Amber Hill, students are rewarded for the number of correct answers they get, not for the acquisition of understanding. In such classrooms it seems unreasonable to expect students to seek difficult and demanding situations which may not lead to correct answers, particularly when correct answers, in a mathematics classroom, have always been the only route to success. Dweck's suggestion that bright girls underachieve because of *maladaptive* tendencies may be seen as an example of blaming the victim (Anyon 1981). One result of this could be that the blame is removed from the school system and focused upon the reported inadequacies of girls. But the tendency to avoid situations which result in failure, taken in the context of high-pressure mathematics classrooms (such as top sets) is not at all maladaptive; in many ways it is eminently sensible. High-pressure environments which expose students when they do not attain correct answers (Buxton 1981) cannot foster a desire in students to seek challenging situations in which they may not succeed:

> *JB*: Can you describe a maths lesson which you haven't enjoyed?
> *L*: Where he was doing something about perimeters of circles and radiuses and that and he picked me out, because I didn't look interested and he was telling me all these things and I had to work it out and I just sat there. I didn't know anything, 'cause I didn't think he explained it and he made me look a fool in front of the whole class, yeah, 'cause I just couldn't speak, 'cause I didn't know what he was talking about and he goes, 'See me after the lesson.'
>
> (Louise, Amber Hill, Year 10, set 1)

The high-pressure environments generated within many mathematics top sets probably encourage and reinforce the tendencies Dweck notes amongst bright girls. It also seems reasonable that girls should become anxious (Tobias 1978) in response to these environments, rather than reposition their goals and replace their desire for understanding with a desire for speed, as many of the boys seemed to have done:

> Some of the stuff you do, it's just hard and some of it's really easy and you can just remember it every time. I mean, sometimes you try and race past the hard bits and get it mostly wrong, to go onto the easy bits that you like.
>
> (Paul, Amber Hill, Year 10, set 1)

In the UK there is evidence that mathematics is taught to setted groups in approximately 94 per cent of schools (Ofsted 1996 reported in *The Guardian* 8 June 1996: 7). I would suggest that the negative attitudes reported amongst bright girls (Dweck 1986) and the inequities present amongst the top 5 per cent of students (Askew and Wiliam 1995) may derive from some of the intrinsic features of top set mathematics classrooms, rather than the personal inadequacies of girls. At Amber Hill the top set girls were clear about the reasons for their disaffection and underachievement and these did not relate to their own shortcomings but to the way in which mathematics was presented to them within their fast and pressured top set classrooms.

Attribution theory

Attribution theory (Ames *et al.* 1977; Ames 1984) has focused upon the anxiety of girls and the tendency of girls to attribute their failure to their own perceived lack of ability. This has been used by psychologists and educationalists to suggest ways in which girls should change, ways in which they should become less anxious, more confident, in essence, more masculine. Anyon (1981) has described a tendency toward 'blaming the victim' and this process is evident in much of the research based upon attribution theory and 'intervention strategies' (Mura 1995: 159).

In such research, the responsibility for change is laid firmly at the feet of the girls. The reasons for their actions are ignored and potential problems with mathematical epistemology and pedagogy are not considered. One of my aims in this chapter is to identify the reasons for the girls' adverse reactions to school mathematics and to give voice to their concerns (see also Boaler 1997a, b). The girls at Amber Hill talked openly about their mathematical anxiety, but they did not attribute this anxiety to any deficiencies of their own. They were quite clear about the reason for their anxiety which was the system of school mathematics that they had experienced.

If we don't understand it, he'll shout at us, call us idiots in other words, but it's his own teaching.

(Helen, Amber Hill, Year 11, set 1)

Every report he writes, he writes 'good ability but lacks confidence', but I know that I can do the work – in a different situation, with a different sort of work.

(Maria, Amber Hill, Year 11, set 1)

The Amber Hill girls clearly attributed their 'underachievement' to the mathematical pedagogy and epistemology they experienced (Burton 1995; Johnston 1995; Mura 1995; Willis 1995) and although many of the girls believed that they were mathematical failures and they demonstrated anxiety in lessons, none of the girls related this to their own perceived inadequacies. They felt that they had been disadvantaged by their school's mathematics teaching and 'in a different situation, with a different sort of work' they could have done well.

Amber Hill: summary

The girls at Amber Hill experienced a real conflict. They believed in the value of understanding and they knew that there was a need to think about work, but their school's approach did not always allow them to do so. When they worked at their own pace, when they worked in groups and when they worked on open-ended projects, they felt able to gain access to understanding. Hence their preference for these approaches. The majority of the boys at Amber Hill also preferred a more open, reflective approach, but in the absence of this they seemed able to adapt to a system that they did not like, but which gave them high marks. The boys were not happy, but they were able to play the game, to abandon their desire for understanding and to race through questions at a high speed. Dweck (1986) has talked about the importance of students' goals to their subsequent success and failure in cognitive performance. It was clear that the goals that the Amber Hill girls formed were almost impossible to achieve in their mathematics lessons and the effect of this conflict upon their regard for mathematics was clear.

Phoenix Park school

The students at Phoenix Park worked co-operatively on projects at all times; they were given the freedom to work in any way that they wanted; they were encouraged to think for themselves; they discussed ideas with each other; and they worked at their own pace. In these respects, the approach at Phoenix Park matched the idealized learning environment represented by the girls at Amber Hill. Not surprisingly perhaps, gender differences were evident amongst the students at Phoenix Park and these worked in favour of the girls. However, these affected a relatively small number of students and they did not result in widespread disaffection and underachievement.

In Chapter 5, I described a group of students, who were mainly boys, who resisted the approach of Phoenix Park. These students related their low motivation to the open approach and, as some of the girls reported in Chapter 5, they wanted more structure in their work; they wanted someone to tell them what to do, 'they didn't want to find things out for themselves' (Anna, Phoenix Park, Year 11). The fact that this response was concentrated amongst a small group of boys suggests that it was gender-based. Martin Collins, the mathematics co-ordinator at Phoenix Park, believed that some of the boys lacked the maturity to take responsibility for their own learning and there was some evidence that this was true. For example, in Year 10 interviews, some of the boys were extremely antagonistic towards the approach, but by the end of Year 11 they were considerably more positive. This may have been due to the fact that they needed time to get used to the demands of an open approach, or that they had simply become more mature by the time they reached Year 11.

The boys that appeared to be disaffected because of the approach at Phoenix Park were in the minority and they demonstrated similar low motivation and bad behaviour in all of their lessons (although most, but not all, of these were project-based). Thus, the gender-based responses at Phoenix Park were very different from those at Amber Hill. At Amber Hill, they were more consistent and widespread and they affected girls who were both successful and motivated in other subject lessons. The disaffection of the boys at Phoenix Park was global, whereas the disaffection of the girls at Amber Hill was local – it related only to mathematics. Also, the girls and boys at Phoenix Park did not develop different perceptions about mathematics. Earlier in this Chapter, I described a Year 10 questionnaire item in which students were asked to rank five different aspects of mathematics in terms of importance. This produced significant gender differences on three of the five mathematical features at Amber Hill and no significant differences at Phoenix Park. I also showed that there were significant differences in the responses of Amber Hill girls and boys to three statements in their Year 11 questionnaire describing different aspects of mathematics. There were no significant differences between the girls and boys on any of these questions at Phoenix Park. This is important because at Amber Hill the girls seemed to value aspects of mathematics teaching and learning which were not present in their school's approach. At Phoenix Park, the views of girls and boys were consistent with the approach they encountered at school.

Further indications of the gender patterns at the two schools were provided by the Year 9 questionnaire. Two of the questions asked students whether they were good at mathematics in school and whether they enjoyed school mathematics. In both of these questions, boys gave more positive responses than girls at Amber Hill and girls gave more positive responses than boys at Phoenix Park. These two questions demonstrate the same pattern (Tables 9.1 and 9.2). At Amber Hill, where students followed a traditional, textbook approach, the boys gave more confident responses and reported enjoying mathematics more than the girls. At Phoenix Park, where school mathematics was open, experiential and discussion-based, the reverse was true: slightly more of the girls gave positive responses than boys but the differences between girls and boys were not significant. The results concerning enjoyment and understanding reported in these Year 9 questionnaires were repeated in Years 10 and 11.

In their Year 9 questionnaire, the students were also asked to write sentences about the aspects of lessons they liked, disliked and would like changed. In response to these three questions there were a total of 88 comments from Amber Hill students about their perceived lack of understanding. The majority of these comments reflected a considerable amount of anxiety and more than two-thirds of the comments were given by girls. At Phoenix Park, there were six comments in response to these three questions that reflected anxiety about understanding, and these came from equal numbers of girls and boys.

In interviews the Phoenix Park girls also gave very different responses to the Amber Hill girls. Many more of the Phoenix Park girls reported enjoying mathematics, and this they related to the fact that they worked in open, non-competitive environments in which they could use their own ideas and think deeply about their work.

Table 9.1 'Do you think you are good, OK or bad at the maths you do in school?'

School	good (%)	OK (%)	bad (%)	n
Amber Hill				
Girls	6	80	13	82
Boys	32	66	1	77
Phoenix Park				
Girls	23	72	5	43
Boys	22	65	13	60

Table 9.2 'Do you enjoy the maths you do in school?'

School	Always/most of the time (%)	Sometimes (%)	Hardly ever/never (%)	n
Amber Hill				
Girls	37	52	11	82
Boys	51	44	5	77
Phoenix Park				
Girls	63	23	14	43
Boys	45	35	20	60

In GCSE examinations, there were significant disparities in the achievements of Amber Hill girls and boys with 20 per cent of the boys and 9 per cent of the girls entered attaining GCSE grades A to C. At Phoenix Park, there were no significant differences in the achievements of girls and boys, with 13 per cent of the boys and 15 per cent of the girls attaining grades A–C. The relatively low proportion of Phoenix Park boys attaining grades A–C, compared with Amber Hill boys, could be taken as an indication that the Phoenix Park approach disadvantaged boys. However, other forms of evidence do not support this view. It seems more likely that the disparity between Phoenix Park's open approach and the GCSE examination, discussed in Chapter 6, diminished the proportion of both girls and boys attaining A–C grades in the examination.

Discussion and conclusion

In concluding this chapter, I would like to draw together a number of points which illuminate or contradict existing theoretical standpoints consistently deployed within education and psychology, relating to girls and mathematics.

1 At Amber Hill school, a large proportion of girls became disaffected by, and disillusioned with, their school mathematics. These girls achieved less than a similar cohort of girls at Phoenix Park and were considerably more disaffected. The girls at Amber Hill were eloquent about the reasons for their disaffection and underachievement and these they related to pace, pressure, and closed approaches which did not allow them to think and a competitive environment. Conversely, they related open work, discussion and co-operation to understanding. Burton (1986a, b, 1995) has proposed that process-based mathematical approaches will raise the achievement, and enjoyment, of girls but, to date, there has been little research evidence to support this.

2 The difference between the achievement of girls and boys at Amber Hill in relation to a traditional, closed approach appeared to relate to their *adaptability* to an approach they disliked. Both sets of students expressed preferences for open, discussion-oriented work but boys adapted to the converse of this, whereas the girls, generally, did not. The boys tended to rush through questions in order to achieve speed, if not understanding. The girls would not do this, they seemed unable to suppress their desire for understanding and continued to strive towards it – which probably worked to their disadvantage.

3 Attribution theory has played an important part within psychological analyses of girls' underachievement in mathematics. Various psychologists have suggested that girls tend to attribute their lack of success to themselves and Dweck (1986) proposes that this leads to a condition known as 'learned helplessness'. Attribution theorists have tended to rely upon experimental evidence to support their claims and it is interesting to contrast this evidence with the reported experiences of girls in *real*, classroom situations. For at the end of five years of secondary schooling, the girls at Amber Hill were

clear about the reasons for their lack of success in mathematics and these had nothing to do with their own inadequacies. The Amber Hill girls found that they were unable to improve their situation, not because they were disillusioned by their own inadequacies, but because they were powerless to change the epistemological and pedagogical traditions of their institution.

4 Dweck (1986: 1040) has analysed the negative reactions of girls to school mathematics and described their responses as 'maladaptive'. I have argued that the girls' responses should be considered in relation to their goals in mathematics and if their goals relate to understanding, which they clearly do, their responses are far from maladaptive. I believe that the work of intervention strategists may have, unwittingly, served to prolong a period, from which we are only now emerging, in which girls' explanations for their own underachievement have been ignored. Burton also argued in 1986 that intervention strategies would be ineffective if they did not attempt to locate and understand the nature of girls' 'problems' from a broad perspective (Burton 1986b). Very few researchers consulted the girls, or listened to their concerns, before labelling them as 'anxious' and sending them on programmes to become more confident. But it is clear to me that the girls' responses to school mathematics make perfect sense. Indeed, their proposals for the improvement of school mathematics are markedly similar to those offered by experienced mathematics educators. They want to be able to understand mathematics and they will not accept a system which encourages rote learning of methods and procedures that mean little or nothing to them.

5 Previous research which has considered the links between sex and learning styles has reported small or negligible effect sizes. This has led educationalists to dismiss any possible differences between girls and boys, partly because it would be dangerous to form expectations on the basis of *presumed* learning styles (Adey *et al.* 1995). However, it seems equally dangerous to ignore sex-based preferences for styles of learning when the teaching approaches that are offered to school students are clearly biased towards one group of students. Mathematics, as it is currently and widely taught, is not equally accessible to girls and boys and this appears to relate to preferences of pedagogy. Many of the psychological studies that have reported negligible learning style differences between girls and boys (see for example, Riding and Douglas 1993) have done so by reducing learning preferences to small measurable concepts related, for example, to a verbal versus imagery approach or a holist versus analyst approach. These are then assessed through closed questionnaires, administered in experimental settings. One of the indications of this research study was that the preferences of girls for open, reflective and discursive approaches that allowed a 'connected' type of thinking (Gilligan 1982; Becker 1995) would not be easily identifiable through experimental tests for learning styles. The preferences of the students at Amber Hill were wider ranging, more complex and, importantly, related to the context of their mathematics lessons. These preferences may well have been 'situation-specific' (Lave 1988) which would have seriously limited their testability in experimental settings.

6 The disparity between preferred modes of working and school mathematics practice was most acute for the highest ability girls at Amber Hill. In recent

years, girls' performance in mathematics has improved dramatically in relation to boys (Elwood *et al.* 1992) and the only real differences that still exist in favour of boys occur amongst the top 5 per cent of students. The disaffection and underachievement which was common amongst the highest ability girls at Amber Hill derived partly from the increased pressure and speed associated with top set environments as well as the increased *awareness* of the girls of the inadequacy of an approach that denied them access to understanding. These girls, more than others, wanted to understand their mathematics and consequently, these girls, more than others, become anxious and underachieved when they were denied the opportunity to do so.

I began this chapter with a quote from Johnston (1995) which suggested that it may be time to listen to the girls who complain about the nature of school mathematics. I have attempted, in this chapter, to show the importance of giving voice to girls' concerns, because what they are saying appears to make a lot of sense. However, it is important not to lay the blame for their disaffection upon mathematics *per se*, for the fault lies not with the intrinsic nature of mathematics, but with school mathematics as it is commonly constructed. Rogers and Kaiser (1995) talk about the need to move away from a paradigm that has blamed girls for the pedagogical and institutional inadequacies of the school system and move towards a new form of school mathematics. At Phoenix Park, the teachers were quite radical in their reconstruction of school mathematics and this seemed to produce an alleviation, or even eradication, of mathematical anxiety and underachievement amongst girls. Importantly, they achieved this by changing the mathematics pedagogy and epistemology, not the girls.

10

Setting, social class and survival of the quickest

Introduction

The appropriateness of setting, streaming and mixed-ability grouping remains a contentious and widely disputed issue within education. This is made more interesting in the UK by the fact that moves from streaming to setting to mixed-ability teaching and back again to setting can be related directly to developments in research, educational theory and the political agendas of the time. In this chapter, I will present a brief overview of the theoretical and historical developments which surround student grouping. I will then consider the influence of ability grouping upon the perceptions and understandings the students developed at Amber Hill and Phoenix Park.

In the 1950s, almost all of the schools in the UK were streamed and students were differentiated within, as well as between, schools. Jackson (1964) conducted a survey of junior schools and found that 96 per cent were streamed and 74 per cent of the schools had placed children into ability groups by the time they were seven years old. Jackson's study also identified some of the negative effects of streaming, including the tendency of teachers to underestimate the potential of working-class children, and the tendency for low-stream groups to be given less-experienced and less-qualified teachers. This report contributed towards an increasing public awareness of the inadequacies of streamed systems. In 1967, the Plowden Report recommended the abolition of all forms of ability grouping in primary schools (Bourne and Moon 1994).

In the 1960s and 1970s both Hargreaves (1967) and Lacey (1970) explored and highlighted the ways in which setting[1] and streaming[2] created and maintained inequalities, particularly for working-class students. Ball (1981) also conducted a highly influential study of a school moving from setting to mixed-ability teaching that served to establish the link between setting and working-class underachievement. Schools appeared to be receptive to the results of these research studies and the 1970s and early 1980s witnessed a growing support for mixed-ability teaching in the UK. This fitted with the more pervasive concern for educational equality at that time.

The 1990s have seen an apparent reversal of this thinking, manifested by large numbers of schools returning to policies of setting (Ofsted 1994). Even within the current political climate such a move must be considered to be remarkable, given that setting was replaced in many schools, less than thirty years ago, because of concerns about issues of equity and disadvantage. Yet the motives behind such moves are easy to locate. As a result of the Education Reform Act 1988, schools in England and Wales have been forced to adopt a highly structured and differentiated national curriculum (Dowling and Noss 1990), a curriculum that many teachers believe is incompatible with mixed-ability teaching (Gewirtz *et al.* 1993). At the same time, schools are now having to spend time, money and energy creating images that will attract the 'right' sort of parents – parents whose children will gain high GCSE grades and secure their school's survival in the newly created educational marketplace (Gewirtz *et al.* 1993). Middle-class parents, who schools particularly want to attract, are thought to favour setted educational systems (Gewirtz *et al.* 1995). The fact that schools are prepared to accept, or ignore, the limitations of setting can also be linked to a notion, held by many people across the education community, that setting raises academic achievement, at least for some students. At its *worst*, setting is believed to enhance the experiences of students in high sets and diminish the experiences of students in low sets. With the current attainment-driven climate of GCSE league tables and high stakes assessments, the attainment of potential A–C students is regarded as more important than the attainment of lower ability students (Gewirtz *et al.* 1995). All of these developments have meant that setting is now back in vogue and schools are returning to policies of differentiation, with its associated polarization (Abraham 1994) in large numbers.

In this Chapter, I aim to increase understanding of the ways in which setting and mixed-ability teaching impact upon understanding (see also Boaler 1997a,c). I will also consider the responses of individual students who were taught in low and high sets and mixed-ability groups and the impact that grouping had upon their perceptions and responses to school. I hope, in this way, to inform theoretical perspectives on student grouping policies and to complete the picture I am presenting of the different factors that influenced students' learning at Amber Hill and Phoenix Park.

The setting experience at Amber Hill

The Amber Hill mathematics department was an interesting place to consider the impact of setting, because the students experienced both mixed-ability and setted approaches within the same school for mathematics, at different times. In Year 7, the students worked through individualized booklets, at their own pace, in mixed-ability groups. In Year 8, they were setted, but continued working through their booklets at their own pace. In Year 9, they changed to a class-taught textbook system. These differences gave the students extremely interesting insights into setted and mixed-ability approaches and it was clear from my case study results that some of the students' responses to their mathematics teaching were related to the setted nature of their experiences. I will now discuss each of these features in turn, starting with the one that seemed to have the most impact upon the largest number of students.

Working at a fixed pace

Probably the main reason that teachers place students into sets in mathematics is so that they can reduce the spread of ability within the class, enabling them to teach mathematical methods and procedures to the entire group, as a unit.

> It's good [setting] because you're putting similar abilities together. I mean it's easier to pitch your lesson, to pitch the work at them, to teach them all together, you know, from the front, as a class.
>
> (Edward Losely)

There is evidence that the way in which teachers proceed in setted lessons is by teaching towards a reference group of students (Dahllöff 1971). Teachers generally pitch their lessons at the middle of the group, on the basis that faster or slower students will be able to adjust to the speed at which lessons are delivered. At Amber Hill, many of the students were unable to make this adjustment and when they changed in Year 9 from working at their own pace to working at a fixed pace, many students became disaffected and their attainment started to decline. The view that working at a fixed pace diminished understanding was prevalent both amongst students who found lessons too fast and students who found lessons too slow. But these were not unusual or extreme students, almost all of the students seemed to find some lessons, or some parts of lessons, either too fast or too slow:

> C: I felt like I was learning – you feel you was learning more, 'cause the teacher would help you – if you went up to him and showed him the book. He would help you and I felt I learned more in the first and second year, but in the fourth and fifth year it's more slow and, like, if you finish first you have to wait for the others, or if you're behind you have to work fast because everyone else is finished.
> M: And that's why I don't like maths any more 'cause I can't go at my own pace.
>
> (Chris and Marco, Amber Hill, Year 11, set 4)

The pace at which students felt comfortable working seemed to be determined by a wide range of factors. These included the difficulty of individual topics, the students' own prior experience, individual preferences and, of course, their feelings on that day.

The fact that Amber Hill used setting did not mean that the teachers *had* to teach students as a group at a fixed pace, but for many teachers the only reason for establishing setted groups is to enable teaching from the front to whole classes. There would be very little point in setting students, given the known disadvantages this confers upon low set students, if the students then worked at their own pace, which they could do in mixed-ability groups. At Amber Hill, the main purpose of setted groups was also the main source of disaffection for the students as well as the factor that almost all students linked with diminished learning opportunities and underachievement.

The students' second major complaint about setting was also related to class teaching, but it extended beyond this. A major concern of significant numbers of students interviewed was the pressure that they felt was created by the existence and form of their setted environments.

Pressure and anxiety

Many of the Amber Hill students, particularly girls, were anxious about mathematics and the students linked their anxiety to the pressure created by setted classes. Some of this pressure derived from the need to work at a pace set by the teacher:

> I don't mind maths but when he goes ahead and you're left behind, that's when I start dreading going to maths lessons.
>
> (Helen, Amber Hill, Year 11, set 1)

> I mean she's rushing through and she's going, 'We've got to finish this chapter by today,' but I'm still on C4 [a textbook exercise] and I don't know what the hell she's chatting about and I haven't done any of it, 'cause I don't know it. She hasn't explained it properly. She just says, 'Take this off, take that off,' and she puts the answers up and like – what? I don't know what she's doing.
>
> (Karen, Amber Hill, Year 11, set 3)

Another aspect of the students' anxiety related to a more reflective pressure. The creation of groups intended to be homogeneous in ability caused many students to feel that they were constantly being judged alongside their peers.

> L: I preferred it when we were in our tutor groups.
> JB: Why?
> L: 'Cause you don't worry so much and feel under so much pressure then, 'cause now you've got people of the same standard as you and they can do the same stuff and sometimes they can do it and you can't and you think, 'Oh, I should do that' and then you can't . . . but if you're in your tutor group you're all a different status . . . it's different.
>
> (Lindsey, Amber Hill, Year 11, set 4)

One of the reasons commonly given for the formation of setted groups is that the competition created by setted classes helps to raise achievement. For some students this was probably true:

> You have to keep up and it actually, in a way it motivates you, you think if I don't do this then I'll get behind in the class and get dropped down a set.
>
> (Gary, Amber Hill, Year 11, set 3)

However, of the 24 students interviewed in Year 11, only one student, Gary, gave any indication that the competition and pressure created by their setted environments enhanced motivation or learning. At Amber Hill, setting was a high-profile concept and the students were frequently reminded of the set they were in. This served as a constant standard against which they were judged and the students gave many indications that this continual pressure was not conducive to their learning.

Top set experiences

Undoubtedly the most intense pressure in mathematics lessons was experienced by students in the top set, and at Amber Hill, placement in the top set appeared to have serious negative consequences for the learning and achievement of some students (Boaler 1997a). Most, but not all, of these students were girls and I described some of the ways in which these girls were disadvantaged by their top set experiences in Chapter 9. The top set of my case study year group was taught by the head of mathematics, Tim Langdon, who was, himself, ambivalent about setting:

> '. . . a lot of people are not prepared to take on board mixed-ability and if I'm speaking as a head of department, I'm obviously trying to look to maximize what people I've got in my department in front of me, so if we move the question on to what I can see, I can see a whole bunch of people who are happy with sets, sets by ability and we'll stick with that and look for making them feel comfortable so they're prepared to give me as much as possible. If, from my own point of view, yes, I would like some mix of ability within a group because I still feel there's some trickle-down effect and still more positive effect within a group with a spread of ability.
>
> (Tim Langdon)

Despite Tim's ambivalence towards the setting process, the environment within his own top set group embodied many of the features which characterize top set mathematics groups, particularly rapidly paced lessons, competition between students and pressure to succeed. In my observations of Tim's top set class, I was often surprised by the pace of the lessons compared with the lessons he taught to other sets. All of the teachers at Amber Hill taught lessons at a pace that I would regard as reasonably fast, but the top set lessons were distinct. The identification of students as 'top set' seemed to set off a whole variety of heightened expectations for the teachers about their learning capabilities. It was almost as if the teachers believed that they were dealing with a completely different sort of student, one that did not experience problems, one which understood the meaning of examples flashed up on the board for a few seconds and one which could rush through questions in a few moments, deriving real meaning from them as they did so. In the extract below, Lorna and Jackie, two of the top set girls, described their lessons to me:

L: So he'll go through, like, notes on the board and go through questions and ask us questions and then . . .

J: Leave us to it.

L: But sometimes, when we've got to get a chapter finished, we go through it *so fast* and sometimes we don't know where we're at, like, what we're supposed to have done, what we're, you know, what's coming up.

J: It feels like the teacher's skipping things but he's not, it's just that we've got to go through it so fast.

L: Yeah, and sometimes you forget what you've done don't you?

J: Yeah.

L: Like you've just taken one thing in and then you've got to switch to the next chapter or the next piece; it's confusing.

J: Yeah, you get really confused.

(Lorna and Jackie, Amber Hill, Year 10, set 1, with the student's own emphasis)

In interviews, the top set students were distinct from students in other groups by virtue of their discourse, in particular, their constant reference to the pace of lessons using words like 'speed', 'zoom', 'fast' and 'whizz':

All we've been doing for weeks is practising exam papers, but even that, you just zoom through it, you can't take your own time to do it, and then, it's when you come to the lesson, he's just zooming through it, and still you can't get it, you don't understand it properly.

(Helen, Amber Hill, Year 11, set 1)

In order to monitor whether the features of Tim's top set teaching were common to other top set groups, taught by other teachers, I started to observe lessons from other year groups. This showed that many of the same features, particularly the speed, pressure and competition, were emphasized in other set 1 classes. Indeed, the top set lessons taught by different teachers seemed to have more in common with each other than with lessons taught by the same teachers to different ability groups. Hilary Neville usually took set 3 or 4 classes but she had one top set group, in Year 7. During my observations of this class, I was struck by the similarity between these lessons and other top set lessons with different teachers and year groups. Hilary seemed to change into a different teacher for these lessons, she treated the students differently and her explanations were very fast. The top set lessons in all the year groups were taught with an air of urgency, almost as though the status of the students meant that the lessons had a completely different agenda to lessons taught to students in other groups. The students also reported that the teachers had very different expectations of them because they were in the top set:

JB: Can you tell me about being in set 1?

H: They expect you to know more.

M: Yeah, they expect too much, it's like, 'Oh you should know this.'

H: You should know that.

M: You're the top set.

M: And he goes *fast*, like, we'll be on one chapter one lesson and the next lesson it'll be, 'We've done enough of that, go onto the next one.'

H: Yeah and it's, Oh my God it's, I mean I know it's the same in every lesson, but they, like, set you so much work in maths and they expect you to definitely have it in by next time, and it's . . . all subjects do that, but, in maths, it's different.

M: It's tough.
H: Yeah, it's tough.

(Helen and Maria, Amber Hill, Year 11, set 1, with the
student's own emphasis)

In questionnaires given to the students when they were in Year 9, I asked them to describe themselves as 'good', 'OK' or 'bad' at the mathematics they did in school. No girls and only two boys in set 1 described themselves as good at mathematics. In their Year 10 questionnaires, the students were asked whether they enjoyed mathematics lessons 'always', 'sometimes' or 'never'. The set 1 students were the most negative group in the year, with the smallest proportion of students' responding 'always' (0 per cent) and the greatest proportion of 'never' (27 per cent; six girls and two boys). Sets 1 and 2 between them contributed over two-thirds of the 'never' ratings from sets 1 to 8 ($n = 163$).

A number of different research studies have linked mathematical enjoyment with mathematical ability or competence. Understandably, students who are good at mathematics tend to enjoy it, whereas students who experience successive failure in mathematics tend to dislike it. At Amber Hill, the top two sets were made up of students who, at one time, were doing well in mathematics. Despite this, the students liked mathematics less than other students and had less confidence in their own ability to do mathematics. For these students, something had clearly gone wrong. During my three years of work at Amber Hill, I became convinced that the negativity of students in set 1 was caused by certain intrinsic features of the set 1 experience. This conviction derived from a number of sources. First, 10 of the 12 students interviewed from set 1 expressed a clear preference for mathematics lessons in Years 7 and 8 when they worked in mixed-ability classes, using an individualized approach:

> 'Cause you learned a lot more [in mixed-ability groups] and you could recap everything which you didn't understand and spend more time on it, but now you've just got to try and whizz and do your best.

(Jackie, Amber Hill, Year 10, set 1)

Second, in questionnaires given to all of the students in Year 10, 17 of the 30 top set students gave comments similar to the ones below:

> The teacher rushes through methods faster than most pupils can cope.

> The lesson is difficult and we work at such a fast pace that I find it hard to keep up.

> I dislike basically everything. The methods of teaching are too fast and confusing.

Third, when in their Year 10 questionnaire, the students were asked to name their best ever mathematics lesson, all the students who described a mathematics lesson ($n = 17$) chose their coursework projects. Nine other students did not give an answer and four students chose a lesson when a policewoman came in to give a talk about weapons. The 17 students who prioritized their coursework lessons over all others said that they did so because they valued the opportunity to work at their own pace, to find things out for themselves and to experience a less confrontational style of learning.

The set 1 students were a group of very committed and able students who should have been enjoying and succeeding at mathematics. Instead, their comments suggest considerable disaffection, particularly because of the speed of lessons and the pressure they experienced. This story of negativity and anxiety was repeated in different top set mathematics groups across Amber Hill school and is a story that, I believe, is repeated in many top set mathematics classrooms across the country for small, but significant, groups of students. When my case study group were in Year 10, I gave a questionnaire to students in Years 9, 10 and 11 ($n = 420$). The set 1 students across the three year groups responded differently from other students on this questionnaire. For example, set 1 students comprised 26 per cent of the students who said that they never enjoyed mathematics, 38 per cent of the students who described lessons as fast and 27 per cent of the students who said that they were always anxious in lessons, when set 1 students made up only 19 per cent of the cohort. On all of these questions, the views of the set 1 students, taught by different teachers, were consistent across the three year groups.

JB: Can you think of some good and bad things about being in set 1?
L: I can think of the bad things.
C: I agree.
JB: OK, what are the bad things?
L: You're expected to know everything, even if you're not sure about things.
C: You're pushed too hard.
L: He expects you to work all the time at a high level.
C: It makes me do less work, they expect too much of me and I can't give it so I just give up.

(Lorna and Carly, Amber Hill, Year 11, set 1)

The students indicated that the nature of their top set environment had diminished their understanding of mathematics. This idea was validated by a number of the different assessments that have been reported so far. Two class groups at Amber Hill were the focus of the long-term learning study. One was a top set Year 9 group; the other a set 4 Year 10 group, both taught by the same teacher – Edward Losely. A comparison of the instances of positive learning where students learned something and remembered it, with instances when they learned something but then forgot it, showed that the Year 9 set 1 group did significantly worse than the mixed-ability Year 9 group at Phoenix Park and the Year 10 set 4 group at Amber Hill. Indeed, in this top set group, 10 out of 22 students, (45 per cent of the group), attained lower scores in the delayed post-test than they did in the pre-test taken before the work was introduced to them. This compared with two students from the Year 9 Phoenix Park group and no student in the Year 10 set 4 group at Amber Hill.

Although this research was of a small scale, it showed quite clearly that the learning of the Year 9 top set students, on the particular piece of work assessed, was extremely ineffective and, for almost half of the group, it may even have been detrimental. Nothing about this work made it distinct from any other piece of work the students did and in my observations of their lessons the students were motivated and worked hard. Edward taught them methods, at the usual pace for the class; the students watched, listened and then practised the methods, as was normal for the school.

The students in my top set case study group also attained the lowest grades, of sets 1 to 4, on both aspects of the applied 'Architectural' activity (pp. 65–8) and the area question in the 'Planning a flat' activity (pp. 68–72). The students in set 1 seemed to have particular difficulty working out what they should do within these assessments, possibly because they had learned methods at a faster pace than other students and were particularly prone to making 'cue-based' decisions in an attempt to get by in lessons. Further indication of the difficulties experienced by top set students was provided by the conceptual and procedural results reported in Chapter 6. These showed that students who took the higher-level examination paper in the top set at Amber Hill were less able than other students to answer conceptual questions and this contrasted strongly with the most able students at Phoenix Park. The top set students showed in three different assessments that their learning of mathematics may have disabled them in a variety of situations.

The third major complaint of the students at Amber Hill was particularly prevalent amongst students outside set 1 and it related to the way in which setting limited their potential opportunities and achievements.

Restricted opportunities

In interviews many of the students at Amber Hill expressed clear feelings of anger and disappointment about what they felt to be unfair restrictions upon their potential mathematical achievement. The students, from a variety of sets and ability ranges, cared about their achievement. They wanted to do well and they were prepared to put effort into their work, but many felt that they had been cheated by the setting system:

L: The thing I don't like about maths is . . . I know because we're in set 4 you can only get a D.

S: Yeah, you can't get any higher than a D.

L: So you don't do as much.

S: Yes, you could work really hard and all you can get is a D and you think, 'Well what's the point of working for a D?'

(Lindsey and Sacha, Amber Hill, Year 11, set 4)

I'm in set 3 and the highest grade I can get is a C . . . it's silly because you can't, maybe I wanted to do A level, 'cause maths is so useful as an A level, but I can't because . . . I can get a C if I really push it, but what's the point?

(Alan, Amber Hill, Year 11, set 3)

A number of the students explicitly linked the restrictions imposed by the set they were in to their own disaffection and underachievement. They reported that they simply could not see any point in working in mathematics for the grades that were available to them:

JB: How would you change maths lessons? If you could do it any way you wanted what would you do?

C: Well, work at your own pace and different books.

JB: How would working at your own pace help?

M: Well, it would encourage people more wouldn't it? They'd know they're going for an A wouldn't they? Like, what's the point of me and Chris working for a D? Why are we gonna work for a D?

C: I'm not saying it's not good a D, but . . .

M: It's *not* good, it's crap, they said to us if we get 100 per cent in our maths we're gonna get a D, well what's the point?

(Chris and Marco, Amber Hill, Year 11, set 4, with the student's own emphasis)

These extracts raise questions about the accuracy of the students' assessments of their own potential but, in many ways, the degree of realism in the students' statements is irrelevant. For what the students clearly highlight is the disaffection they felt because of their setting arrangements. The students may have been unrealistic, but the disaffection they experienced because of their restricted attainment was real.

S: We're more to the bottom set so we're not expected to enjoy it.

JB: Why not?

S: I'm not putting, I'm not saying 'cause we're in the lower set we're not expected to enjoy it . . . it's just . . . you're looking at a grade E and then you put work in towards that . . . you're gonna get an E and there's nothing you can do about it and you feel like . . . What's the point in trying, you know? What's the difference between an E and a U?

JB: How did you feel about maths before you were put into sets?

K & S: Better.

(Simon and Keith, Amber Hill, Year 11, set 7)

These feelings of despondency were reported from students in set 3 downwards, and many of the students suggested that the limits placed upon their attainment had caused them to give up on mathematics. The students believed that they had been restricted, unfairly and harmfully, by their placement into sets.

The fourth and final response that prevailed amongst students primarily affected the students in low sets and this related to the way in which the sets were chosen.

Setting decisions

Many of the students interviewed did not feel that the set that they had been put into was a fair reflection of their ability:

I was alright in the first year, but like me and my teacher had a few problems, we didn't get on, that's why I think it's really better to work really hard in the first years, 'cause that's when you've got a chance to prove a point, you know, that you're good and then in the second year you'll end up in a good set and from then on you can work. But me in the first year, I got dumped straight into the bottom set. And I was like, 'Huh? What's going on?,' you know? And they didn't teach me anything there and I was trying hard to get myself up, but I couldn't, 'cause once you're in the bottom it's hard to get up in maths. That's another bad thing about it, and other people now, there's people now in, like, higher sets man and they just know nothing, they know nothing.

(Simon, Amber Hill, Year 11, set 7)

Some of the students, particularly the boys, felt the set they were in reflected their behaviour more than their ability:

Yes but they're knocking us down on our behaviour. Like, I got knocked down from second set to bottom set and now, because they've knocked me down, they've thrown me out of my exams and I know for a fact that I could've got in the top A, B or C.

(Michael, Amber Hill, Year 11, set 7)

Tomlinson (1987) provides evidence that the behaviour of students can influence the examination groups which they are put into and some of the Amber Hill students were convinced that their behaviour, rather than their ability, had determined their mathematics set, which in turn, had partly determined their examination grade.

Amber Hill: summary

The students at Amber Hill were coherent in their views about setting. The 24 students interviewed in Year 11 were in general agreement about the disadvantages they perceived and all but one of the students interviewed expressed strong preferences for mixed-ability teaching. This was because setting, for many of the students, meant one or more of:

- a lack of understanding, when the pace of lessons was too fast;
- boredom when the pace of lessons was too slow;
- anxiety, created by the competition and pressure of setted environments;
- disaffection related to the restricted opportunities they faced; and
- perceived discrimination in setting decisions.

It was also clear from the students that setting did not have a single influence that affected all students in the same way. Some students were probably advantaged by setted lessons, but others had been negatively affected by processes of setting. In almost all cases, the disadvantages students reported concerned their learning of mathematics and their subsequent achievement. Nevertheless, some students also experienced other negative repercussions:

K: You walk around the school and you get people in the top set and you get people in our set and if you walk round the school and you're talking about maths, they put you down because you're not in that set, it's like . . .

S: They're dissing [showing disrespect] you, and that.
K: They're saying you haven't got the ability they've got.

(Keith and Simon, Amber Hill, Year 11, set 7)

Despite the labelling associated with setting, the major concern for the majority of students interviewed was the consequences setting might have for their achievement. In the next section, I shall present various forms of data that give some indication of the way in which the students' achievement was affected by their placement in sets.

Setting and achievement

The students' different responses to setting, given in interviews, indicate that the success or failure of a student in a setted group related to their preferred learning style and their responses to competition, pressure and opportunity (or lack of it). Various quantitative indicators add support to the idea that success was strongly related to factors other than ability. For example, at Amber Hill, there was a large disparity between the attainment of students when they entered setted lessons and their success in GCSE examinations at the end. This may be demonstrated through a consideration of the students' scores on their NFER tests at the end of Year 8 and their scores on their GCSE examinations at the end of Year 11. This information is provided for both of the schools, providing an insight into the different implications of setted and mixed-ability teaching for students' achievement.

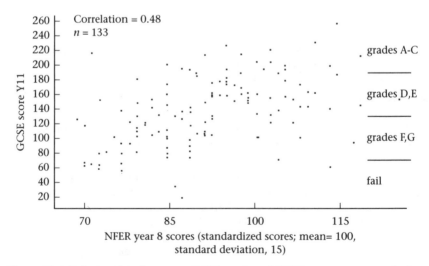

Figure 10.1 Relationship between GCSE mark and NFER entry scores at Amber Hill. See note in Figure 10.2

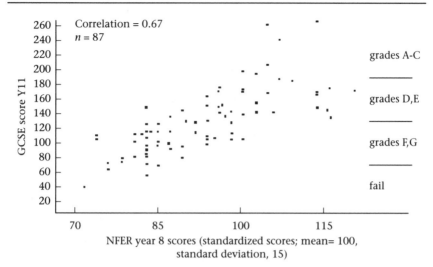

Figure 10.2 Relationship between GCSE grade and NFER entry scores at Phoenix Park

At Amber Hill, a high correlation would be expected between NFER results at the end of Year 8 and eventual achievement, because the students were setted largely on the basis of their NFER results and, once inside their sets, the range of their attainment was severely restricted. At Phoenix Park, a smaller correlation would be expected, because prior to their NFER tests the students had attended fairly traditional middle schools. At Phoenix Park, they experienced considerable freedom to work if and when they wanted to in lessons which, combined with the openness of the school's teaching approach, may have meant that some students would not perform at the end of Year 11 as would be expected from their performance at the end of Year 8. A comparison of performance, before and after setting and mixed-ability teaching at the two schools is shown in Figures 10.1 and 10.2. These scatter-graphs display an interesting phenomenon. They show that at Amber Hill there was a relatively weak relationship between the students' attainment in Year 8 and their eventual success, after three years of working in setted lessons, demonstrated by a correlation of $r = 0.48$. This meant that some students did well, even though indications in Year 8 were that they were not particularly able and some students did badly, despite being high achievers at the end of Year 8. At Phoenix Park, where students were taught in mixed-ability groups and given considerably more freedom, there was a significantly higher correlation of $r = 0.67$ between initial and eventual attainment. These results support the idea that once inside a setted group, a number of factors that are relatively independent of initial attainment influence a student's success.

A second interesting phenomenon was revealed at Amber Hill through a consideration of the relationship between social class and the set into which students were placed. This relationship was examined at both schools because the students were put into setted examination groups at Phoenix Park in the middle of Year 11. Partial correlations from the two schools enable the impact of 'ability' (measured via NFER tests) and social class upon the sets students were given, to be considered. These showed that at Amber Hill there was a significant correlation between the social class of students and the set they were placed into ($r = 0.25$), after controlling for ability, with students of a 'low' social class being more likely to appear in a low set. A similar analysis of partial correlations at Phoenix Park showed that there was a small, but significant, *negative* correlation between social class and examination group ($r = -0.15$), after controlling for ability. This showed that at the end of their mixed-ability teaching experiences, there was a small tendency for students of a 'lower' social class to be placed into a higher examination group at Phoenix Park, than middle-class students of similar initial attainment.

Further insight into the possibility of class bias at Amber Hill is demonstrated by locating individuals at the two schools who achieved more or less than would have been expected from their initial entry scores. At Amber Hill, approximately 20 per cent of the students ($n = 22$) could be described as 'outliers' on the scattergraph. The 22 most extreme outliers on the graph were made up of seven 'overachievers' and 15 'underachievers'. Closer examination of these students gives the sex and class profiles that are illustrated in Tables 10.1 to 10.4. These tables show that amongst the 'overachievers', three-quarters of the students were middle-class, and they were mainly boys. In contrast, only one-fifth of the 'underachievers' were middle-class. These outliers represent only a small proportion of the students at Amber Hill but they show

Table 10.1 Amber Hill students achieving above expectation according to social class* and initial entry score

Gender	Middle class			Working class		
	1	2	3	4	5	6
Girls			1			1
Boys		4	1	1		

* Social class categories based on OPCS classification

Table 10.2 Amber Hill students achieving below expectation according to social class* and initial entry score

Gender	Middle class			Working class		
	1	2	3	4	5	6
Girls			2	4	1	2
Boys	1			5		

* Social class categories based on OPCS classification

Table 10.3 Phoenix Park students achieving above expectation according to social class* and initial entry score

Gender	Middle class			Working class		
	1	2	3	4	5	6
Girls					1	
Boys		1	1	4		

* Social class categories based on OPCS classification

Table 10.4 Phoenix Park students achieving below expectation according to social class* and initial entry score

Gender	Middle class			Working class		
	1	2	3	4	5	6
Girls		1	2	1		
Boys		1	1	2	1	2

* Social class categories based on OPCS classification

quite clearly that those students who did better than would be expected from their initial ability scores tended to be middle-class boys, whereas those who did worse tended to be working-class students (of either sex). This is interesting to contrast with the most extreme 20 per cent of Phoenix Park students ($n = 18$). These students did not 'underachieve' or 'overachieve' to the same extent as the Amber Hill students, as can be seen from the scattergraphs. However, the students who were nearest to the edges of the graph did not reveal any class polarization in achievement at Phoenix Park. Tables 10.3 and 10.4 show that less than one-third of the 'overachievers' at Phoenix Park were middle-class and the 'underachievers' were made up of similar proportions of middle-class and working-class students.

What these results indicate is that, at Amber Hill, the disparity between initial mathematical capability and eventual achievement shown on the scattergraph is partly created by a small number of mainly middle-class students who achieved more than would be expected and a relatively large number of mainly working-class students who achieved less than would be expected, given their attainment on entry to the school. Similar evidence of class polarization is not apparent at Phoenix Park. This quantitative analysis enables social class to be added to the list of factors that appeared to influence achievement in setted lessons. It also re-establishes the notion that success in a setted environment had little to do with 'ability'. The influence of class bias over setting decisions is well documented (Ball 1981; Tomlinson 1987) and some of the students gave some indications, in interviews, about the way that this process may have taken effect. In the following extract, Simon, a working-class student, talked about the way in which he opted out of the 'game' of impressing the mathematics teacher:

> Yes, and in a way, right, when I came to the school, I was scared to ask questions man, so I just thought, 'No forget it, man.'
>
> (Simon, Amber Hill, Year 11, set 7)

This withdrawal because of Simon's fear probably served to disadvantage him when setting decisions were made. The disproportionate allocation of working-class students to low sets shown by the correlations at Amber Hill would certainly have restricted the achievement of working-class students. However, it seems likely that the social class of students may also have affected the way in which individuals responded to the experiences of setted lessons. In the next section, I will attempt to draw together the various results that have been reported so far, in order to illuminate the different factors that influence a student's achievement in setted and mixed-ability groups.

In any debate about the implications of setted and mixed-ability grouping, it is important to consider the achievement of students. The approaches of Amber Hill and Phoenix Park schools differed in many important ways but the GCSE results reported in Chapter 6 show that the setted classes did not achieve better results than the mixed-ability classes, despite the increased time spent 'working' by the Amber Hill students. The students who learned mathematics in an open environment in mixed-ability classes, achieved significantly more A–G grades, than the comparable cohort of students taught in setted groups.

Discussion and conclusion

At Phoenix Park school, the students experienced a great deal of freedom to work when they wanted to work and talk or wander about when they did not. The students were grouped in mixed-ability classes, the more able students were not placed in high sets that would push them, the less able students were not placed in sets in which teachers could concentrate upon their individual needs. At the end of three years of this relaxed and open approach, the students who did well were those of a high ability. Students who did exceptionally well, compared to their entry scores, were mainly working-class students; those who did exceptionally badly were both working-class and middle-class students.

In all of these respects, Amber Hill differed from Phoenix Park and although setting and mixed-ability teaching was not the main focus of my research study, there were a number of clear indications from various forms of data, that at Amber Hill:

- social class influenced setting decisions resulting in disproportionate numbers of working-class students being allocated to low sets;
- significant numbers of students experienced difficulties working at the pace of the class, resulting in disaffection and reported underachievement;
- students became disillusioned and demotivated by the limits placed upon their achievement within their sets;

- some students responded badly to the pressure and competition of setted lessons, particularly girls and students in top sets.

For a student, being able and hard working at Amber Hill was not a guarantee of success within their setted classrooms. Indeed, the students indicated that success depended more upon working quickly, adapting to the norms for the class and thriving upon competition than anything else. A number of different results from this study cast doubt upon some widespread beliefs about setted teaching. For example, there was no qualitative or quantitative evidence that setting raised achievement, but there was evidence that setting diminished achievement for many students. A comparison of the most able students at the two schools showed that the students achieved more in the mixed-ability classes of Phoenix Park than the high sets of Amber Hill (3 per cent of the Phoenix Park cohort gained A* or A grades, compared with 0.5 per cent of Amber Hill's cohort). This could be related to a number of features of the two schools' approaches, but there were many indications from the top set students at Amber Hill that features of their top set learning had diminished their achievement. The various forms of data also seem to expose an important fallacy upon which many setting decisions are based. Students of a similar 'ability', assessed via some test of performance, will not necessarily work at the same pace, respond in the same way to pressure or have similar preferences for ways of working. Grouping students according to ability and then teaching towards an imaginary model student who works in a certain way at a certain pace, will almost certainly disadvantage students who deviate from the ideal model. The stress and anxiety reported by the students in interviews at Amber Hill is probably an indication of this phenomenon.

There was much evidence that the students who were disadvantaged by the setted system of Amber Hill were predominantly working class, female or very able. The class polarization that existed at Amber Hill and that was completely absent at Phoenix Park is consistent with the results of other research studies that have considered the links between setting and class bias (Hargreaves 1967; Lacey 1970; Ball 1981; Tomlinson 1987; Abraham 1995).

A common feature that links all of the findings of this study concerns the individual nature of students' responses to setting. Students at Amber Hill responded to setting in a variety of different ways indicating that it is too simplistic to regard the effects of setting as universally good or bad for all students, even students in the same set. The various quantitative studies that have compared the group scores of setted and mixed-ability classes overlook this fact and, in doing so, overlook the complexity of the learning process for different individuals.

To conclude, *survival of the quickest* may not be the most accurate way to describe the experiences of setted students, for this research has indicated that it was the students who were most able to adapt to the demands of their set who were most advantaged, or least disadvantaged by setting. In predicting who those students may be, it seems fair to assume that if a student is middle class, confident, thrives on competition and pressure and is motivated, regardless of limits on achievement, they will do well in a setted system. For the rest of the students, success will probably depend upon their ability to adapt to a model of learning and a pace of working which is not the most appropriate for their development of understanding.

In the Second International Mathematics Survey of eight countries (Burstein 1993), it was found that the countries that had the most setting were those with the lowest achievement and the countries that had the least setting, or set students at the latest possible time, had the highest achievement. The author of this study (*ibid.*: 306) concluded that setted systems were 'inefficient (they miss a substantial number of talented students) and biased (they favour a social elite). The mechanisms for sorting apparently are seriously flawed, producing unintended outcomes of dubious value'. Despite such evidence many educationalists persist in the idea that setting raises attainment. Approximately 94 per cent of upper secondary mathematics classrooms are setted and evidence is now suggesting that students as young as five or six years are being put into ability groups for mathematics (Brown 1995). In England and Wales there is also a widespread concern about the 'long tail' of underachievers (Reynolds and Farrell 1996) in mathematics. This research study has suggested that the high proportion of low attainers in mathematics in England and Wales may be linked to the high proportion of students taught in setted groups. The Amber Hill students taught in low sets were quite clear that they had given up on mathematics because of the restrictions their low sets placed upon their potential attainment.

The consequences of setting and streaming decisions are great. Indeed, the set or stream that students are placed into, at a very young age, will almost certainly dictate the opportunities they receive for the rest of their lives. It is now widely acknowledged in educational and psychological research that students do not have a fixed 'ability' that is determinable at an early age. However, the placing of students in academic groups often results in the fixing of their potential achievement. Slavin (1990) makes an important point in his analysis of research in this area. He notes that as mixed-ability teaching is known to reduce the chances of discrimination, the burden of proof that ability grouping is preferable must lie with those who claim that it raises achievement. Despite the wide range of research studies in this area, this proof has not been forthcoming.

Notes

1 When students are put into groups according to their perceived ability for individual subject areas.
2 Where students are placed into one 'ability' group that they stay in for all of their subjects.

11

Reflections and conclusions

New theories of learning and situated cognition

In this book, I have attempted to tell the story of the mathematics teaching and learning in two schools, Amber Hill and Phoenix Park. There are a number of theoretical perspectives that might be used to explain or interpret the findings from these schools. For example, the two approaches could be taken as examples of constructivist and non-constructivist teaching, or as exemplifications of problem-solving and computational approaches to mathematics. I have chosen to analyse the results from the perspective of situated cognition because this provides a framework that addresses the way individuals deal with different situations. The breadth of this framework was fundamental in understanding why students used mathematics in one setting and not another and why they appeared to have knowledge, but did not always choose to use it. The findings of this study, interpreted within this framework, illustrate the inherent complexity of the learning process and, crucially, that it is wrong to believe that assessments merely indicate whether a student has *more* or *less* knowledge. Interpretations of learning, knowledge and assessment need to include consideration of the different forms of knowledge that learners possess, the goals they set for themselves in different situations and the ways in which they understand and perceive settings.

At Amber Hill, many of the students appeared to be disadvantaged in the face of new or 'applied' situations. This seemed to be due to a combination of the students' perceptions about mathematics, their understanding of mathematics and the goals they formed in different settings. The Amber Hill students believed that mathematical success required memory, rather than thought. They had developed a shallow and procedural knowledge that was of limited use in new and demanding situations, and their desire to interpret cues and do the 'right thing' suppressed their ability to interpret situations holistically or mathematically. Lave (1988) and Lave and Wenger (1991) have proposed that notions of transfer cannot explain the way individuals use knowledge in different settings because transfer theories do not take account of the 'communities of practice' in which people operate. The results of this study support this view on a number of different levels. For example, the Amber Hill students regarded the mathematical classroom as a highly specialized community of practice unrelated to all others. This idea was formed in response to various aspects of their school setting, such as the formalized nature of the mathematics they encountered, the lack of social interaction in their classrooms and the imposition of school rules. These all encouraged the students to locate their mathematical knowledge within the four walls of their mathematics classrooms. At Phoenix Park, the boundaries between school and the 'real world' were less distinct. This appeared to stem from a number of specific features of the school's approach, including the fact that students were encouraged to use mathematics in order to solve the problems that *they* themselves had posed.

A second important difference between the students at the two schools also relates to Lave's relational view of learning (Lave 1993, 1996a) and it concerns the students' interpretation of mathematical situations. When the Phoenix Park students encountered a mathematical problem, they believed that they should consider the different variables present and then develop ideas in relation to the specific setting in which they found themselves. They were not disabled by the need to try and remember relevant algorithms. When the students described their use of mathematics, they talked about the importance of thought, the adaptation of methods they had learned and their interpretation of different situations. Some students specifically challenged the idea that they would remember a piece of knowledge from their lessons. Instead they described the ways in which they took ideas from lessons and re-formed them in response to different situations. Thus, their descriptions were inconsistent with notions of transfer but entirely consistent with Lave's 'relational' view of learning. At the start of this research study, I set out to establish and monitor the factors that affected students' ability to 'transfer' their learning. I now support Lave's view that this is an inappropriate way to conceptualize the way individuals use mathematics in different settings and this conviction partly derives from the Phoenix Park students' descriptions of their learning and partly from the behaviours of the students at the two schools. Resnick (1993: 3) has claimed that we are currently 'in the midst of multiple efforts to merge the social and the cognitive' and we are witnessing a radical reconstruction of the way that learning is viewed. The reports of the Amber Hill and Phoenix Park students seem to add support to the new, relational idea of knowing that is emerging from this perspective (Resnick 1993; Lave 1993, 1996a).

Gendered styles of learning

The results from the Amber Hill and Phoenix Park case studies both support and challenge different gender perspectives within the field of education. At Amber Hill many of the girls underachieved in mathematics, they demonstrated anxiety and they were disaffected. But the girls did not 'attribute' the 'blame' to themselves. They offered coherent accounts of their desire to understand mathematics and the ways in which they believed their school's textbook approach denied them access to understanding. The girls were clear that their mathematical understanding would have been enhanced if they had been given more opportunity to work in an open way, at their own pace and in groups. Various authors have proposed that intervention strategies be used to try and change girls, in order that they may fit into a fixed model of mathematics teaching (Rogers and Kaiser 1995, develop this point). The girls' comments at Amber Hill supported the idea that equity in mathematics education is more likely to be achieved if mathematical epistemologies and pedagogies are changed (Burton 1986a, 1995). This argument is given further support by the fact that the open, process-based approach at Phoenix Park avoided the development of under achievement and anxiety amongst girls.

'Traditional' and 'progressive' teaching

Ball describes the Conservative vision for education as one in which desks are 'in rows, the children silent, the teacher "at the front", chalk in hand, dispensing knowledge' (Ball 1993: 209). This vision, which is increasingly consistent with the education policies of 'New Labour', is perfectly represented by the mathematics classrooms at Amber Hill. In these classrooms, there was an emphasis upon order and control, the learning of specified, mathematical methods, 'chalk-and-talk' transmission teaching, with children divided into eight narrow bands of 'homogeneous' ability. This research study has demonstrated that each of these traditional features of Amber Hill's mathematics teaching disadvantaged some students in some ways. This was not because the teachers were incompetent or lacked commitment. It arose from the pedagogical, philosophical and epistemological models embraced by the teachers. The teachers at Amber Hill believed in giving students structured pieces of mathematical 'knowledge' to learn, in line with what Ball (1993: 205) has called the 'curricular fundamentalism' of the Conservatives. The teachers did not perceive a real need to give students the opportunity to think about, use or discuss mathematics. Sigurdson and Olson (1992) note that many teachers consider learning and understanding to be synonymous and, because of this, much of school learning is done at rote level. The Amber Hill teachers fitted into this model – they did not see any real difference between a clear transmission of knowledge and student understanding. Most of the problems experienced by the Amber Hill students derived from this knowledge transmission approach, a central feature that shaped mathematics teaching at the school. Other traditional features of the students' environment, such as setting and high-pressure learning, served to exacerbate their problems, but it was the transmission of closed pieces of knowledge that formed the basis of the students' disaffection, misunderstandings and underachievement.

The term 'progressive' is a label that is often used in a pejorative way to describe supposedly ineffective teaching approaches. The Phoenix Park approach was based upon principles of independence and self-motivation and such a label does not begin to reflect the complexity of the different characteristics which constituted the school's approach. However, I have chosen to adopt this term to describe the combination of the school's different features, partly in order to juxtapose the Phoenix Park approach with the 'back to basics' movement and partly because Phoenix Park school embraced many of the principles that traditionalists most fear when they talk about progressive education. At Phoenix Park, the students were schooled in a totally different way from the students at Amber Hill and although the most obvious result of the school's 'progressivism' and lack of imposed order was classrooms that many would describe as chaotic, the results from this study have shown that the students learned more effectively than the Amber Hill students. The Phoenix Park students reported that they developed self-motivation and self-discipline as a result of the school's approach, that the openness of their work encouraged them to think for themselves and the need to use mathematics in different activities caused them to be adaptable and flexible in their approach to mathematics. The general lack of school rules also seemed to produce students who were confident and creative in their response to different situations. Whilst it was the traditional features of Amber Hill school's teaching that appeared to disadvantage their learning, it was the progressive features of Phoenix Park school that served to create students who were generally confident, creative and flexible. The students at Phoenix Park were less constrained and confined and this seemed to have had a significant positive impact upon the way in which they viewed situations and took decisions.

I do not wish to imply that Phoenix Park represented an ideal learning environment; it clearly did not, but a consideration of the ways in which lessons could have been improved did not suggest a move towards the Amber Hill model of teaching. For example, limited classroom observations might suggest that more of the students at Phoenix Park could be encouraged to work, but the students at both schools showed quite clearly that merely making them work did not improve their learning. Students at Phoenix Park worked when they chose to but they still achieved more than the disciplined students at Amber Hill. All of these findings indicate that the most important aim for teachers should be to engage students and to provide worthwhile activities that they find stimulating. This is supported by the work of Bell (1993), who found that intensity and degree of engagement were more important than time on task. High levels of intensity are impossible to maintain all the time, but the Phoenix Park students at least experienced real engagement for some of their school lives. When Mickey and Ahmed, reported in Chapter 5, discovered the way in which they could use trigonometry in order to find an area, they were genuinely interested and excited. The contrast between this and the Amber Hill students' learning of trigonometry could not be more extreme. The findings of this research indicate that lessons in both schools would be improved if students experienced this sort of excitement and engagement more often. But the key to this improvement has to be the design of appropriate activities and the creation of stimulating work environments, not a simple increase in discipline and order. Thus if Phoenix Park's mathematics approach were to be improved this would require a reaffirmation of this 'progressive' principle, not a move towards a traditionalist control and transmission model.

Setting and mixed-ability teaching

The setting of students into homogeneous ability groups is a central part of Conservative and, more recently, Labour party education policies (*The Times*

Educational Supplement 14 June 1996: 7; *The Guardian* 8 June 1996). Such policies do not only concern students in secondary schools. In 1993 all primary schools were sent reports from both the National Curriculum Council (1993) and the Department for Education (circular 16/93) which explicitly encouraged them to introduce or re-introduce setting. The main reason that is generally given for the use of setting is that it raises achievement, particularly for students in high sets. Yet many of the students in high sets at Amber Hill, in a number of different year groups, suffered because of their placement in these higher groups. The teachers of these groups were not particularly authoritarian or supporters of competitive approaches to schooling, but the environments generated within their top set classrooms still induced extreme anxiety amongst many of the students. The 'top set effect' that the students described did not affect all students equally. It served to discriminate at least partly on the basis of sex and a large proportion of the girls in the top set underachieved because of setting. Speed, pressure and competition are all features of classrooms that are implicitly encouraged by Conservative education policies as ways of bringing about higher attainment. For the students at Amber Hill, these policies encouraged misunderstanding and a hatred of mathematics and, in the GCSE examination, they resulted in lower grades than might have been possible in different circumstances. But the disadvantages linked to setting did not affect only students in the top sets. Students throughout the setting spectrum reported that their learning was diminished by having to work at the pace of the whole class, as well as the restrictions placed upon their learning opportunities and potential achievement by the setting structure and its role in curricular differentiation. This did not disadvantage all of the students; some students were probably advantaged by setting, but the picture was very much more varied than proponents of setting lead people to believe. Within this research study, success in a setted mathematics group was not simply determined by mathematical ability or motivation but also by social class, sex, confidence and the ability to adapt to an imposed pace of working.

Twenty-first century thought

Noss (1991, 1994) regards the encouragement of flexibility and adaptability as the most important role for mathematics education in the future, as a necessary response to the development of technologies of various kinds and the changing nature of the job market. The Amber Hill teachers emphasized control and order in their classrooms and encouraged students to follow specified methods and rules. These features of pedagogy and classroom management were, in many ways, incompatible with critical thought and analysis. The students at Amber Hill were not flexible or adaptable in their approach: they did not think critically in mathematical situations and they demonstrated passive, unchallenging acquiescence in lessons. These behaviours appeared to be a direct result of school conditioning towards conformity, order and obedience, an acceptance of school and mathematical rules, and a dependence upon the structures provided by these rules. One of the results of this dependency was that the students were extremely well behaved throughout their mathematics lessons. A more important result was that they lacked critical thought and this certainly disadvantaged them in unfamiliar situations that required their use of mathematics.

In the UK, the Conservative Government of the early 1990s encouraged such 'basic' tenets of education as knowledge transmission, setting and control and order; at the same time they continued to spend money on programmes that were intended to increase the capabilities of school leavers in relation to the 'needs' of the economy. These policies were unstable and contradictory: in stressing both a concern for and emphasis on 'basics', related to knowledge and conformity, they reduced the ability of schools to produce flexible workers capable of initiative. At Amber Hill, it was the very mathematical and school characteristics that were encouraged, implicitly and explicitly by the Conservative Government's reforms of the time, that produced the antithesis of the type of understanding, critical thought and reasoning most needed by school leavers moving into the twenty-first century.

The 'falling standards' debate

Mathematics education has recently taken a leading role within public debates in response to claims of falling standards, poor performance in international studies and badly prepared university students (London Mathematical Society 1995; *Panorama* 3 June 1996). Such reports have re-opened debates about the relative advantages of traditional, 'back to basics' approaches to teaching as against the 'progressive' methods, which are commonly cited as culprits in these accounts. But these debates rarely draw upon any evidence or research. A number of different research projects within mathematics education have contrasted open, progressive or meaning-based approaches to mathematics teaching with closed, traditional, algorithmic approaches (Resnick 1990; Maher 1991; Sigurdson and Olson, 1992; Keedy and Drmacich 1994). These studies have *all* shown that progressive approaches to teaching result in increased attainment, even on traditional tests that are not directly compatible with the teaching approaches used. Athappilly *et al.* (1983) conducted a meta-analysis, which summarized thirty years of experiments comparing modern and traditional mathematics teaching. This analysed the results of 134 controlled-outcome studies and found that 'the average person receiving some form of modern mathematics treatment is 0.24 standard deviations in achievement and 0.12 standard deviations in attitude above an average student not receiving modern mathematics' (Athappilly 1983: 491).

These studies cast serious doubts upon the claim that progressive mathematics education has lowered achievement, a claim that is made even more untenable by a consideration of the way mathematics is commonly taught. A large body of international research (Peterson and Fennema 1985; Romberg and Carpenter 1986) and a range of HMI reports from this country (1985, 1992, 1994) have shown that Amber Hill's mathematics approach was not at all unusual. Sigurdson and Olson (1992) report that most of school mathematics learning is rote and most mathematics tests assess low-level mathematical procedures. Peterson (1988) reports that the majority of mathematics teaching is focused upon the teaching and learning of basic facts and algorithmic procedures and Cheek and Castle (1981) question whether the term 'back to basics' can be applied to mathematics education when evidence shows that a basic approach was never abandoned by the majority of mathematics teachers. They point to research that has shown that 'mathematics instruction has changed little over the past 25 years, despite the innovations advocated' (1981: 264) and that a single textbook continues to be the main source of content in mathematics lessons, with the majority of instruction occurring from the front, followed by the rehearsal of methods in numerous exercises. HMI inspections have shown that most teachers are essentially cautious and conservative (Bolton 1992) and various forms of evidence indicate that this description can be more accurately applied to teachers of mathematics than any other subject group. All of this leads to the conclusion that if mathematical performance is lower than that of other subjects, this is more likely to be due to the traditionalism rather than the progressivism of mathematics teachers.

The various findings of this study offer a bleak view of the learning of the students at Amber Hill, but the research evidence reviewed above suggests that the Amber Hill approach is fairly typical for mathematics. My observations of mathematics classrooms over the last ten years would support this. Jaworski (1994: 8) also notes that in twelve years of teaching mathematics in different parts of this country, the 'exposition and practice' approach was the most common. If the Amber Hill teachers were particularly unusual, it would seem unlikely that all eight of the teachers in the department would share the same 'unusual' characteristics, yet the eight different mathematics teachers, who varied in popularity and experience, prompted the same set of responses from students. In the latest international comparison of 39 countries, England came 38th, above only France, in the proportion of teachers who believed that being able to think creatively is important in mathematics, and 49 per cent of the English students surveyed in the study believed that success in mathematics involved memorizing the textbook (Beaton *et al.* 1996). The only distinctive feature that I noted at Amber Hill was the tendency of the teachers to make mathematics even more closed and rule-bound because of the working-class nature of the students. This tendency to move mathematics into a closed domain served to demonstrate even more clearly the implications of a 'back to basics' approach for learning.

The impact of the GCSE examination

The findings of this study should also prompt consideration of the value of the examination system and the knowledge assessed within it in this country. At Phoenix Park, the school was successful in giving students a broad perspective on mathematics, and the students had become open, flexible thinkers. All this changed when they reached Christmas of Year 11 and they started examination preparation. At this time, they narrowed their view of mathematics, they thought that the new mathematical procedures they were learning were confusing and irrelevant and they constructed barriers or boundaries (Siskin 1994; Lave 1996a) between the mathematical knowledge of the classroom and the mathematical demands of their jobs and lives. Lerman (1990) states that new forms of learning require new forms of assessment and it was obvious that the Phoenix Park students were disadvantaged by an examination system that was incompatible with their school's approach, even though they attained higher grades than the Amber Hill students. More generally, the demands upon all teachers to prepare students for an examination that assesses mathematical methods and procedures, in narrow and closed questions, diminishes the potential for teachers to move away from a narrow and closed teaching model and reduces the likelihood of their spending time letting students explore and use mathematics in open or authentic situations.

Prior to the start of my research study, Phoenix Park was involved in a pilot of a new examination that combined open and closed questions, in order to assess mathematical process as well as content. In 1994, the School Curriculum and Assessment Authority withdrew this new form of GCSE examination. The next cohort of Phoenix Park students was required to take the more traditional content-based examination. The proportion of students attaining grades A–C and A–G shifted from 32 per cent and 97 per cent, respectively, in 1993 to 12 per cent and 84 per cent, respectively, in 1994. In the summer following the end of my three-year research project, Phoenix Park was inspected by Ofsted. In anticipation of this inspection and the need to increase GCSE grades, the head teacher at Phoenix Park forced the mathematics department to end their project-based approach and teach from textbooks. In response to the new middle-class parents putting pressure upon the school, Phoenix Park also started to set students for mathematics. The teachers in the mathematics department responded badly to these changes with feelings of demoralization and disempowerment. Jim Cresswell was convinced that the students were being disadvantaged in many ways and that the changes would not increase examination performance, particularly for students in low set groups who, he reported, had become disaffected. Jim believed that he was ineffective as a textbook teacher and he has now left the teaching profession. Significantly, he believed that there was no place for an open, authentic approach to mathematics education within the 'back to basics' political climate of the time.

Generalizing from this study

I have made some fairly strong and controversial claims in this book and questions are bound to be raised about their generalizability. Some will argue that the disaffection and underachievement that the students experienced at Amber Hill were related to intrinsic features of Amber Hill school and can therefore be ignored. Questions about the generalizability of the study will, of course, be raised, but the detail of the study and the students' own accounts of their learning should provide readers with sufficient information to base their decisions about factors of importance at the two schools. This is part of the value of ethnographic accounts; they do not provide multiple instances of the same phenomenon, but they provide the detail for readers to decide for themselves about the relevance of the reported experiences to their own settings. In conducting this study, I became convinced that the disadvantages faced by students at Amber Hill school were not specific to that school. I also became convinced that it would be wrong to ignore the messages given by the students at Amber Hill and Phoenix Park. The scarcity of the type of mathematical environment encouraged at Phoenix Park make the students' reported experiences from this school particularly important. The messages that emerged from the two schools go against the current tide of anti-'progressive' public opinion and associated drives to increase the formalization of mathematics teaching, but this must surely make these messages important to consider at this time.

I suggested at the start of this book that the evidence for the generalizability of the research would be found within the pages that followed. This was a study of only two schools, but the messages that emerged from the two schools were extraordinarily consistent. The idea that traditional models of teaching disadvantaged students did not come from my own predispositions or from individual students' descriptions. It came from the repeated reports of students, which were supported by observations in lessons, questionnaires and various different assessments. Importantly, the accounts presented here do not rest upon a single data type or even a single research paradigm. The primary elements of the analysis were made even more persuasive by the fact that they were consistent across the different teachers at Amber Hill and even across the two schools.

My main concern in this study has been with the nature and form of the processes which influence students in classrooms. In order to address this I employed both qualitative and quantitative methods and my claims for rigour rest upon the triangulation of different methods, sources of data, sources of accounts and research results. It has been fortunate for this research, although clearly not for the students, that the Amber Hill approach had an extreme impact on the students, because it helped to crystallize the problems of the approach and to isolate those features which influenced the students' responses to mathematics. But the reason I was able to investigate the factors of importance at the two schools was the flexibility that was provided by an ethnographic framework. Research in mathematics education has been dominated by quantitative techniques and methods for many years. This study has indicated, I hope, the potential of multi-method, ethnographic accounts in documenting and understanding different aspects of students' experiences. Some people will inevitably challenge the results of this research and attribute them to factors which have not been discussed, but part of the value and power of ethnographic methods is the flexibility they allow researchers to consider and investigate the importance of different factors in a holistic and exhaustive fashion. After hundreds of hours spent in the classrooms at the two schools, after hearing the students' own accounts of their learning, after analysing over 200 questionnaire responses each year and after consideration of the results of various different assessments, I feel confident that I have been able to identify the main factors that were and were not influential in the students' development of understanding. The findings of this research indicate that the differences between the schools do not rest simply upon good or bad teaching, but upon the potential of open and closed teaching approaches for the development of different forms of knowledge.

Implications for the future

The students who left Amber Hill and Phoenix Park at the end of my research had developed very different capabilities and understandings as a result of their school training. At Amber Hill, many of the students were submissive, unlikely to think mathematically in situations they would encounter and generally disillusioned by their mathematical experiences. At Phoenix Park, many of the students were confident, they liked to use their initiative and they were flexible in their use of mathematics. These responses can be related back to the mathematical and whole-school approaches they experienced. Phoenix Park's mathematics department has now moved a long way towards the Amber Hill model of teaching and there is evidence that many other schools are returning to policies of setting and textbook teaching in response to Government initiatives. Perhaps the most worrying result of this trend is that there no longer seems to be a place in English schools for teachers who want to innovate or try new approaches or strive towards something more than examination training. Jim Cresswell was forced to leave teaching because he did not know of any school that taught mathematics using an open approach, despite the enormous wealth of research evidence, spanning over sixty years, that has shown the advantages of these approaches (Benezet 1935a,b, 1936; Charles and Lester 1984; Baird and Northfield 1992; Cobb *et al.* 1992). Schools in England and Wales now have to teach the same curriculum and most of them have adopted the same traditional pedagogy and practice, because they believe that this is what is required by the National Curriculum and the examination system. Phoenix Park's open, project-based approach has been eliminated and there is a real possibility that the students who left the school in 1995 as active mathematical thinkers will soon be replaced by students of mathematics who are submissive and rule-bound and who see no use for the methods, facts, rules and procedures they learn in their school mathematics lessons:

S: If we do use maths outside of school it's got the same atmosphere as how it used to be, but not now.

JB: What do you mean by it's 'got the same atmosphere'?

S: Well, when we used to do projects, it was like that, looking at things and working them out, solving them – so it was similar to that, but it's not similar to this stuff now, it's, you don't know what this stuff is for really, except the exam.

(Sue, Phoenix Park, Year 11)

References

Abraham, J. (1994) Positivism, structurationism and the differentiation – polarisation theory: a reconsideration of Shilling's novelty and primacy thesis. *British Journal of Sociology of Education*, 15(2): 231–41.

Abraham, J. (1995) *Divide and School: Gender and Class Dynamics in Comprehensive Education*. London: Falmer Press.

Adey, P., Fairbrother, R., Johnson, B. and Jones, C. (1995) A Review of Research Related to Learning Styles and Strategies. Unpublished report prepared for Ofsted. London: Ofsted.

Ames, C. (1984) Achievement attributions and self-instructions under competitive and individualistic goal structures. *Journal of Educational Psychology*, 76: 478–87.

Ames, C., Ames, R. and Felker, D. W. (1977) Effects of competitive reward structure and valence of outcome on children's achievement attributions. *Journal of Educational Psychology*, 69: 1–8.

Anyon, J. (1980) Social class and the hidden curriculum of work. *Journal of Education*, 162(1): 67–92.

Anyon, J. (1981) Schools as agencies of social legitimation. *International Journal of Political Education*, 4(3): 195–218.

Askew, M. and Wiliam, D. (1995) *Recent Research in Mathematics Education 5–16*. London: HMSO.

Athappilly, K., Smidchens, U. and Kofel, J. (1983) A computer-based meta-analysis of the effects of modern mathematics in comparison with traditional mathematics. *Education Evaluation and Policy Analysis*, 5(4): 485–93.

Baird, J. R. and Northfield, J. R. (eds) (1992) *Learning from the PEEL Experience*. Melbourne: Monash University.

Ball, S. J. (1981) *Beachside Comprehensive*. Cambridge: Cambridge University Press.

Ball, S. J. (1987) *The Micro-Politics of the School*. Methuen: London.

Ball, S. J. (1993) Education, Majorism and the curriculum of the dead. *Curriculum Studies*, 1(2): 195–214.

Ball, S. J. (1995) Intellectuals or technicians? The urgent role of theory in educational studies. *British Journal of Educational Studies*, 43(3): 255–71.

Barnes, D., Britton, J., Rosen, H. and the London Association of Teachers of English (1969) *Language, the Learner and the School*. Harmondsworth: Penguin.

Becker, J. R. (1995) Women's ways of knowing in mathematics, in P. Rogers and G. Kaiser (eds) *Equity in Mathematics Education: Influences of Feminism and Culture*, pp. 163–74. London: Falmer Press.

Beaton, A. E., Mullis, I. V. S., Martin, M. O., Gonzalez, E. J., Kelly, D. L. and Smith, T. A. (1996) *Mathematics Achievement in the Middle School Years: IEA's Third Mathematics and Science Study*. Chestnut Hill, Massachusetts: Boston College.

Belencky, M. F., Clinchy, B. M., Goldberger, N. R. and Tarule, J. M. (1986) *Women's Ways of Knowing: The Development of Self, Voice and Mind*. New York: Basic Books.

Bell, A. W. (1993) Some experiments in diagnostic teaching. *Educational Studies in Mathematics*, 24(1): 115–37.

Benezet, L. P. (1935a) The teaching of arithmetic. I. The story of an experiment. *Journal of the National Education Association*, November: 241–4.

Benezet, L. P. (1935b) The teaching of arithmetic. II. The story of an experiment. *Journal of the National Education Association*, December: 301–3.

Benezet, L. P. (1936) The teaching of arithmetic. III. The story of an experiment. *Journal of the National Education Association*, December: 241–4.

Bernstein, B. (1966) Sources of consensus and disaffection in education. *Journal of the Association of Assistant Mistresses*, 17(1): 4–11.

Bernstein, B. (1971) On the classification and framing of educational knowledge, in M. F. D. Young (ed.) *Knowledge and Control*, pp. 47–69. London: Butler and Tanner.

Bernstein, B. (1975) Class and pedagogies: visible and invisible, in B. Bernstein (ed.) *Class, Codes and Control. Volume 3: Towards a Theory of Educational Transmissions*, pp. 116–45. London: Routledge and Kegan Paul.

Beynon, J. (1985) *Initial Encounters in the Secondary School*. London: Falmer Press.

Blum, W. and Niss, M. (1991) Applied mathematical problem solving, modelling, applications and links to other subjects – state, trends and issues in mathematics instruction. *Educational Studies in Mathematics*, 11(1): 37–69.

Boaler, J. (1996) Learning to lose in the mathematics classroom: a critique of traditional schooling practices in the UK. *Qualitative Studies in Education*, 9(1): 17–33.

Boaler, J. (1997a) When even the winners are losers evaluating the experiences of 'top set' students. *Journal of Curriculum Studies*, 29(2): 165–82.

Boaler, J. (1997b) Reclaiming school mathematics: the girls fight back. *Gender and Education*, 9(3).

Boaler, J. (1997c) Setting, social class and survival of the quickest. *British Educational Research Journal*.

Boaler, J. (1998) Open and closed mathematics approaches: student experiences and understandings. *Journal of Research in Mathematics Education*, 29(1): 41–62.

Bolton, E. (1992) The quality of teaching, in Network Educational Press (ed.) *Education – Putting the Record Straight*. Stafford: Network Press.

Bourne, J. and Moon, B. (1994) A question of ability?, in B. Moon and A. Mayes (eds) *Teaching and Learning in the Secondary School*, pp. 25–37. London: Routledge.

Brousseau, G. (1984) The crucial role of the didactical contract in the analysis and construction of situations in teaching and learning mathematics, in H. G. Steiner (ed.) *Theory of Mathematics Education*, pp. 110–19. Bielefeld, Germany: Institut für Didactik der Mathematik der Universität Bielefeld.

Brown, M. (1995) Validity and impact of national tests in the primary school: the teacher's view. Paper presented at BERA Conference, Bath University, September 1995.

Brown, J., Collins, A. and Duguid, P. (1989) Situated cognition and the culture of learning. *Educational Researcher*, 18(1): 32–42.

Burstein, L. (1993) *The IEA Study of Mathematics. III: Student Growth and Classroom Processes*. Oxford: Pergamon Press.

Burton, L. (1986a) Femmes et Mathematique: y-a-t'il une intersection? Paper presented to the *Femmes et Mathematiques*. Conference, Quebec, Canada, June.

Burton, L. (1986b) (ed.) *Girls Into Maths Can Go*. Eastbourne: Holt, Rinehart.

Burton, L. (1995) Moving towards a feminist epistemology of mathematics, in P. Rogers and G. Kaiser (eds) *Equity in Mathematics Education: Influences of Feminism and Culture*, pp. 209–26. London: Falmer Press.

Buxton, L. (1981) *Do You Panic About Maths?: Coping with Maths Anxiety*. London: Heinemann Educational Books.

Charles, R. and Lester, Jr, F. (1984) An evaluation of a process-oriented instructional program in mathematical problem solving in grades 5 and 7. *Journal for Research in Mathematics Education*, 15(1): 15–34.

Cheek, H. and Castle, K. (1981) The effects of back-to-basics on mathematics education. *Contemporary Educational Psychology*, 6: 263–77.

Cobb, P. (1986) Contexts, goals, belief and learning mathematics. *For the Learning of Mathematics*, 6(2): 2–10.

Cobb, P., Wood, T., Yackel, E. and Perlwitz, M. (1992) A follow-up assessment of a second-grade problem-centered mathematics project. *Educational Studies in Mathematics*, 23: 483–504.

Cockcroft, W. H. (1982) *Mathematics Counts: Report of Inquiry into the Teaching of Mathematics in Schools*. London: HMSO.

Cognition and Technology Group at Vanderbilt (1990) Anchored instruction and its relationship to situated cognition. *Educational Researcher*, 19(6): 2–10.

Corrigan, P. (1979) *Schooling the Smash Street Kids*. Basingstoke: Macmillan.

Dahllöf, U. (1971) *Ability Grouping, Content Validity and Curriculum Process Analysis*. New York: Teachers' College Press.

Delamont, S. (1984) The old girl Network: reflections on the fieldwork at St Luke's, in R. Burgess (ed.) *The Research Process in Educational Settings: Ten case studies*. London: Falmer Press.

Department for Education (1993) *DFE News 16/93. Improving Primary Education – Patten*. London: DFE.

Diener, C. I. and Dweck, C. S. (1978) An analysis of learned helplessness: continuous changes in performance, strategy and achievement cognitions following failure. *Journal of Personality and Social Psychology*, 36: 451–62.

Dowling, P. and Noss, R. (eds) (1990) *Mathematics versus the National Curriculum*. London: Falmer Press.

Doyle, W. (1983) Academic work. *Review of Educational Research*, 53(2): 159–99.

Doyle, W. (1988) Work in mathematics classes: the context of students' thinking during instruction. *Educational Psychologist*, 23(2): 167–80.

Doyle, W. and Carter, K. (1984) Academic tasks in classrooms. *Curriculum Enquiry*, 14: 129–49.

Dweck, C. S. (1986) Motivational processes affecting learning. *American Psychologist* (Special Issue: Psychological science and education), 41(10): 1040–8.

Eisenhart, M. (1988) The ethnographic research tradition and mathematics education research. *Journal for Research in Mathematics Education*, 19(2): 99–114.

Elwood, J., Hayden, M., Mason, K., Stobart, G. and White, J. (1992) *Differential Performance in Examinations at 16+: English and Mathematics*. London: SEAC.

Erlwanger, S. H. (1975) Case studies of children's conceptions of mathematics. Part 1. *Journal of Children's Mathematical Behaviour*, 1(3): 157–283.

Fletcher, C., Caron, M. and Williams, W. (1985) *Schools on Trial: The Trials of Democratic Comprehensives*. Milton Keynes: Open University Press.

Gewirtz, S., Ball, S. and Bowe, R. (1993) Values and ethics in the education market place: the case of Northwark Park. *International Studies in Sociology of Education*, 3(2): 233–54.

Gewirtz, S., Ball, S. and Bowe, R. (1995) *Markets, Choice and Equity in Education*. Buckingham: Open University Press.

Gibson, J. J. (1986) *The Ecological Approach to Visual Perception*. Hillsdale, NJ: Lawrence Erlbaum.

Gilligan, C. (1982) *In a Different Voice: Psychological Theory and Women's Development*. Cambridge, MA: Harvard University Press.

Glaser, B. G. and Strauss, A. L. (1967) *The Discovery of Grounded Theory: Strategies for Qualitative Research*. New York, NY: Aldine.

Graded Assessment in Mathematics (1988) *GAIM Development Pack*. London: Macmillan.
Greeno, J., Smith, D. and Moore, J. (1993) Transfer of lituated learning, in D. Detterman and R. Sternberg (eds) *Transfer on Trial*, pp. 99–167. Norwood, NJ: Ablex.
Hammersley, M. (1992) *What's wrong with Ethnography?: Methodological Explorations*. London: Routledge.
Hargreaves, D. (1967) *Social Relations in a Secondary School*. London: Routledge and Kegan Paul.
Head, J. (1995) Gender identity and cognitive style. Paper presented at UNESCO/ULIE Colloquium 'Is there a Pedagogy for Girls?' London: UNESCO.
Her Majesty's Inspectorate (1985) *Mathematics from 5 to 16*. London: HMSO.
Her Majesty's Inspectorate (1992) *Mathematics Key Stages 1, 2 and 3*. London: HMSO.
Her Majesty's Inspectorate (1994) *Mathematics Key Stages 1, 2 and 3*. London: HMSO.
Hiebert, J. (1986) *Conceptual and Procedural Knowledge: The Case of Mathematics*. Hillsdale, NJ: Lawrence Erlbaum.
Hiebert, J. and Carpenter, T. (1992) Learning and teaching with understanding, in D. A. Grouws (ed.) *Handbook of Research on Mathematics Teaching and Learning*, pp. 65–100. New York: Macmillan.
Holt, J. (1967) *How Children Learn*. Harmondsworth: Penguin.
Huberman, A. M. and Crandall, D. P. (1982) Fitting words to numbers. *American Behavioural Scientist* 26(1): 62–83.
Jackson, B. (1964) *Streaming: An Education System in Miniature*. London: Routledge and Kegan Paul.
Jaworski, B. (1994) *Investigating Mathematics Teaching: A Constructivist Enquiry*. London: Falmer Press.
Johnston, B. (1995) Mathematics: an abstracted discourse, in P. Rogers and G. Kaiser (eds), *Equity in Mathematics Education: Influences of Feminism and Culture* pp. 226–34. London: Falmer Press.
Keddie, N. (1971) Classroom knowledge, in M. F. D. Young (ed.) *Knowledge and Control*, pp. 133–60. London: Collier-Macmillan.
Keedy, J. and Drmacich, D. (1994) The collaborative curriculum at the school without walls: empowering students for classroom learning. *The Urban Review*, 26(2): 121–35.
Kluckhohn, F. (1940) The participant observation technique in small communities. *American Journal of Sociology*, 46(3): 331–43.
Lacey, C. (1970) *Hightown Grammar*. Manchester: Manchester University Press.
Lampert, M. (1986) Knowing, doing and teaching multiplication. *Cognition and Instruction*, 3: 305–42.
Lave, J. (1988) *Cognition in Practice*. Cambridge: Cambridge University Press.
Lave, J. (1993) Situating learning in communities of practice, in L. Resnick, J. Levine and T. Teasley (eds) *Perspectives on Socially Shared Cognition*, pp. 63–85. Washington: American Psychological Association.
Lave, J. (1996a) 'Situated Cognition in Mathematics'. Seminar held at Oxford University, Department of Educational Studies, 3 May 1996.
Lave, J. (1996b) Personal communication.
Lave, J. and Wenger, E. (1991) *Situated Learning: Legitimate Peripheral Participation*. New York: Cambridge University Press.
Lave, J., Murtaugh, M. and de la Rocha, O. (1984) The dialectical construction of arithmetic practice, in B. Rogoff and L. J (eds) *Everyday Cognition: Its Development in Social Context*, pp. 67–97. Cambridge, Massachusetts: Harvard University Press.
Leacock, E. B. (1969) *Teaching and Learning in City Schools*. New York: Basic Books.
Lerman, S. (1990) Alternative perspectives of the nature of mathematics and their influence on the teaching of mathematics. *British Educational Research Journal*, 16(1): 53–61.

London Mathematical Society, Institute of Mathematics and its Applications and Royal Statistical Society (1995) *Tackling the Mathematics Problem*. London: London Mathematical Society.

Maher, C. (1991) Is dealing with mathematics as a thoughtful subject compatable with maintaining satisfactory test scores? A nine-year study. *Journal of Mathematical Behaviour*, 10: 225–48.

Masingila, J. (1993) Learning from mathematics practice in out-of-school situations. *For the Learning of Mathematics*, 13(2): 18–22.

Mason, J. (1989) Mathematical abstraction as the result of a delicate shift of attention. *For the Learning of Mathematics*, 9(2): 2–9.

Miles, M. B. (1982) A mini cross site analysis [Commentary on other studies]. *American Behavioural Scientist*, 26(1): 121–32.

Mura, R. (1995) Feminism and strategies for redressing gender imbalance in mathematics, in P. Rogers and G. Kaiser (eds) *Equity in Mathematics Education: Influences of Feminism and Culture*, pp. 155–62. London: Falmer Press.

National Council for Teachers of Mathematics (1989) *Curriculum and Education Standards for School Mathematics*. Virginia: NCTM.

National Curriculum Council (1993) *The National Curriculum at Key Stages 1 and 2: Advice to the Secretary of State for Education*. York: NCC.

Neill, A. S. (1985) *Summerhill*. Harmondsworth: Penguin.

Noss, R. (1991) The social shaping of computing in mathematics education, in D. Pimm and E. Love (eds) *Teaching and Learning School Mathematics*, pp. 205–19. London: Hodder and Stoughton.

Noss, R. (1994) Structure and ideology in the mathematics curriculum. *For the Learning of Mathematics*, 14(1): 2–11.

Nunes, T., Schliemann, A. D. and Carraher, D. W. (1993) *Street Mathematics and School Mathematics*. New York: Cambridge University Press.

Ofsted (Office for Standards in Education) (1994) *Mathematics Key Stages 1, 2, 3 and 4*. Her Majesty's Stationery Office: London.

OPCS (Office of Population Censuses and Surveys) (1980) *Classification of Occupations 1980*. London: HMSO.

Panorama (1996) 'Hard Lessons'. BBC1, 3 June 1996. London: British Broadcasting Corporation.

Perry, M. (1991) Learning and transfer: instructional conditions and conceptual change. *Cognitive Development*, 6(4): 449–68.

Peterson, P. (1988) Teaching for higher order thinking in mathematics: the challenge for the next decade, in D. Grouws and T. Cooney (eds) *Effective Mathematics Teaching*, pp. 2–26. Reston, Virginia: Lawrence Erlbaum.

Peterson, P. and Fennema, E. (1985) Effective teaching, student engagement in classroom activities and sex-related differences in learning mathematics. *American Educational Research Journal*, 22(3): 309–35.

Peterson, P. L. and Swing, S. R. (1982) Beyond time on task: students' reports of their thought processes during classroom instruction. *The Elementary School Journal*, 82(5): 481–91.

Resnick, L. (1990) From protoquantities to number sense, in G. Booker, P. Cobb and T. Menduciti (eds) *Proceedings of the Fourteenth PME Conference, Mexico*, pp. 305–11. Caxtepex, July.

Resnick, L. B. (1993) Shared cognition: thinking as social practice, in L. B. Resnick, J. M. Levine and S. D. Teasley (eds) *Perspectives on Socially Shared Cognition*, pp. 1–22. Washington, DC: American Psychological Association.

Reynolds, D. and Farrell, S. (1996) *Worlds Apart? A Review of International Surveys of Educational Achievement Involving England*. London: HMSO.

Riding, R. and Douglas, G. (1993) The effect of cognitive style and mode of presentation on learning performance. *British Journal of Educational Psychology*, 63: 297–307.

Rogers, P. and Kaiser, G. (eds) (1995) *Equity in Mathematics Education: Influences of Feminism and Culture*. London: Falmer Press.

Romberg, T. A. and Carpenter, T. A. (1986) Research on teaching and learning mathematics: two disciplines of scientific inquiry, in M. C. Wittrock (ed.) *Handbook of Research on Teaching*, pp. 850–73. New York: Macmillan.

Rosenbaum, J. E. (1976) *Making Inequality: The Hidden Curriculum of High School Tracking*. New York: Wiley.

Schoenfeld, A. (1992) Learning to think mathematically: problem solving, meta-cognition, and sense making in mathematics, in D. A. Grouws (ed.) *Handbook of Research on Mathematics Teaching and Learning*, pp. 334–71. New York: Macmillan.

Schoenfeld, A. H. (1985) *Mathematical Problem Solving*. New York: Academic Press.

Schoenfeld, A. H. (1988) When good teaching leads to bad results: the disasters of 'well-taught' mathematics courses. *Educational Psychologist*, 23(2): 145–66.

Sharp, R. and Green, A. (1975) *Education and Social Control: A Study in Progressive Primary Education*. Boston, Massachusetts: Routledge and Kegan Paul.

Sigurdson, S. and Olson, A. (1992) Teaching mathematics with meaning. *Journal of Mathematical Behaviour*, 11: 37–57.

Siskin, L. S. (1994) *Realms of Knowledge: Academic Departments in Secondary Schools*. London: Falmer Press.

Slavin, R. E. (1990) Achievement effects of ability grouping in secondary schools: a best evidence synthesis. *Review of Educational Research*, 60(3): 471–99.

Strauss, A. and Corbin, J. (1990) *Basics of Qualitative Research: Grounded Theory Procedures and Techniques*. Newbury Park, CA: Sage.

The Guardian (1996) 'Blair rejects mixed ability teaching'. 8 June 1996: 7.

Times Educational Supplement (1996) 'Don't give idealism a bad name'. 14 June 1996: 7.

Tobias, S. (1978) *Overcoming Math Anxiety*. New York: Norton.

Tomlinson, S. (1987) Curriculum option choices in multi-ethnic schools, in B. Troyna (ed.) *Racial Inequality in Education*, pp. 92–108. London: Tavistock.

Treffers, A. (1987) *Three Dimensions: A Model of Goal and Theory Description in Mathematics Instruction – the Wiskobas Project*. Dordrecht, The Netherlands: Kluwer.

Walker, R. and Adelman, C. (1975) *A Guide to Classroom Observation*. London: Methuen.

Whitehead, A. N. (1962) *The Aims of Education*. London: Ernest Benn.

Willis, P. (1977) *Learning to Labor*. New York: Columbia University Press.

Willis, S. (1995) Gender reform through school mathematics, in P. Rogers and G. Kaiser (eds) *Equity in Mathematics Education: Influences of Feminism and Culture*, pp. 186–99. London: Falmer Press.

Young, M. F. (1993) Instructional design for situated learning. *Educational Technology, Research and Development*, 41(1): 43–58.

Index

MARKETS, CHOICE AND EQUITY IN EDUCATION

Sharon Gewirtz, Stephen J. Ball and Richard Bowe

- What has been the impact of parental choice and competition upon schools?
- How do parents choose schools for their children?
- Who are the winners and losers in the education market?

These important and fundamental questions are discussed in this book which draws upon a three year intensive study of market forces in education. The authors carefully examine the complexities of parental choice and school responses to the introduction of market forces in education. Particular attention is paid to issues of opportunity and equity, and patterns of access and involvement related to gender, ethnicity and social class are identified.

This is the first comprehensive study of market dynamics in education and it highlights the specificity and idiosyncrasies of local education markets. However, the book is not confined to descriptions of these markets but also offers a systematic theorization of the education market, its operation and consequences. It will be of particular interest to students on BEd and Masters courses in education, headteachers and senior managers in schools, and policy analysts.

Contents
Researching education markets – Choice and class: parents in the marketplace – An analysis of local market relations – Managers and markets: school organization in transition – Schooling in the marketplace: a semiological analysis – Internal practices: institutional responses to competion – Choice, equity and control – Glossary of terms – References – Index.

224pp   0 335 19369 2 (Paperback)   0 335 19370 6 (Hardback)